Praise for *Boardwalk Empire and Philosophy* . . .

"Prohibition was more than just the illegalization of alcohol—it encouraged the majority of the population to disregard the law. The culture of Prohibition—jazz music, radio, fashion, and speakeasies—is the backdrop to a TV drama that raises deep philosophical questions about how we live our lives today. Boardwalk Empire and Philosophy *uses the fictional world of Nucky Thompson to confront these issues in a fascinating way."*

> — CLINT JONES, philosophy teacher, University of Kentucky

"Bootlegging mobsters, crooked politicians, cute flapper girls, federal agents, and assorted riffraff can all be found schmoozing and kvetching about Life at the speakeasy known as Boardwalk Empire and Philosophy. *Let our 200-proof team of philosophers make it so everclear how much your lives have in common with theirs. You'll be surprised!"*

> — JOHN V. KARAVITIS, CPA, MBA, pop culture blogger and financial analyst

"Martin Scorsese's very sober look at this incredible time in American history can help us understand the events and values that shaped the America we know. Boardwalk Empire and Philosophy *ranges from the essence of happiness and the American Dream to the morality of lying and the nature of truth itself. Instead of two thumbs up, I give it two 'bottoms up'!"*

> — ABROL FAIRWEATHER, Professor of Philosophy, San Francisco State University

Boardwalk Empire and Philosophy

Popular Culture and Philosophy® Series Editor: George A. Reisch

VOLUME 1 *Seinfeld and Philosophy: A Book about Everything and Nothing* (2000)

VOLUME 2 *The Simpsons and Philosophy: The D'oh! of Homer* (2001)

VOLUME 3 *The Matrix and Philosophy: Welcome to the Desert of the Real* (2002)

VOLUME 4 *Buffy the Vampire Slayer and Philosophy: Fear and Trembling in Sunnydale* (2003)

VOLUME 5 *The Lord of the Rings and Philosophy: One Book to Rule Them All* (2003)

VOLUME 9 *Harry Potter and Philosophy: If Aristotle Ran Hogwarts* (2004)

VOLUME 12 *Star Wars and Philosophy: More Powerful than You Can Possibly Imagine* (2005)

VOLUME 13 *Superheroes and Philosophy: Truth, Justice, and the Socratic Way* (2005)

VOLUME 19 *Monty Python and Philosophy: Nudge Nudge, Think Think!* (2006)

VOLUME 25 *The Beatles and Philosophy: Nothing You Can Think that Can't Be Thunk* (2006)

VOLUME 26 *South Park and Philosophy: Bigger, Longer, and More Penetrating* (2007)

VOLUME 30 *Pink Floyd and Philosophy: Careful with that Axiom, Eugene!* (2007)

VOLUME 31 *Johnny Cash and Philosophy: The Burning Ring of Truth* (2008)

VOLUME 33 *Battlestar Galactica and Philosophy: Mission Accomplished or Mission Frakked Up?* (2008)

VOLUME 34 *iPod and Philosophy: iCon of an ePoch* (2008)

VOLUME 35 *Star Trek and Philosophy: The Wrath of Kant* (2008)

VOLUME 36 *The Legend of Zelda and Philosophy: I Link Therefore I Am* (2008)

VOLUME 37 *The Wizard of Oz and Philosophy: Wicked Wisdom of the West* (2008)

VOLUME 38 *Radiohead and Philosophy: Fitter Happier More Deductive* (2009)

VOLUME 39 *Jimmy Buffett and Philosophy: The Porpoise Driven Life* (2009) Edited by Erin McKenna and Scott L. Pratt

VOLUME 41 *Stephen Colbert and Philosophy: I Am Philosophy (And So Can You!)* (2009) Edited by Aaron Allen Schiller

VOLUME 42 *Supervillains and Philosophy: Sometimes, Evil Is Its Own Reward* (2009) Edited by Ben Dyer

VOLUME 43 *The Golden Compass and Philosophy: God Bites the Dust* (2009) Edited by Richard Greene and Rachel Robison

VOLUME 44 *Led Zeppelin and Philosophy: All Will Be Revealed* (2009) Edited by Scott Calef

VOLUME 45 *World of Warcraft and Philosophy: Wrath of the Philosopher King* (2009) Edited by Luke Cuddy and John Nordlinger

Volume 46 *Mr. Monk and Philosophy: The Curious Case of the Defective Detective* (2010) Edited by D.E. Wittkower

Volume 47 *Anime and Philosophy: Wide Eyed Wonder* (2010) Edited by Josef Steiff and Tristan D. Tamplin

VOLUME 48 *The Red Sox and Philosophy: Green Monster Meditations* (2010) Edited by Michael Macomber

VOLUME 49 *Zombies, Vampires, and Philosophy: New Life for the Undead* (2010) Edited by Richard Greene and K. Silem Mohammad

VOLUME 50 *Facebook and Philosophy: What's on Your Mind?* (2010) Edited by D.E. Wittkower

VOLUME 51 *Soccer and Philosophy: Beautiful Thoughts on the Beautiful Game* (2010) Edited by Ted Richards

VOLUME 52 *Manga and Philosophy: Fullmetal Metaphysician* (2010) Edited by Josef Steiff and Adam Barkman

VOLUME 53 *Martial Arts and Philosophy: Beating and Nothingness* (2010) Edited by Graham Priest and Damon Young

VOLUME 54 *The Onion and Philosophy: Fake News Story True, Alleges Indignant Area Professor* (2010) Edited by Sharon M. Kaye

VOLUME 55 *Doctor Who and Philosophy: Bigger on the Inside* (2010) Edited by Courtland Lewis and Paula Smithka

VOLUME 56 *Dune and Philosophy: Weirding Way of the Mentat* (2011) Edited by Jeffery Nicholas

VOLUME 57 *Rush and Philosophy: Heart and Mind United* (2011) Edited by Jim Berti and Durrell Bowman

VOLUME 58 *Dexter and Philosophy: Mind over Spatter* (2011) Edited by Richard Greene, George A. Reisch, and Rachel Robison-Greene

VOLUME 59 *Halo and Philosophy: Intellect Evolved* (2011) Edited by Luke Cuddy

VOLUME 60 *SpongeBob SquarePants and Philosophy: Soaking Up Secrets Under the Sea!* (2011) Edited by Joseph J. Foy

VOLUME 61 *Sherlock Holmes and Philosophy: The Footprints of a Gigantic Mind* (2011) Edited by Josef Steiff

VOLUME 62 *Inception and Philosophy: Ideas to Die For* (2011) Edited by Thorsten Botz-Bornstein

VOLUME 63 *Philip K. Dick and Philosophy: Do Androids Have Kindred Spirits?* (2011) Edited by D.E. Wittkower

VOLUME 64 *The Rolling Stones and Philosophy: It's Just a Thought Away* (2012) Edited by Luke Dick and George A. Reisch

VOLUME 65 *Chuck Klosterman and Philosophy: The Real and the Cereal* (2012) Edited by Seth Vannatta

VOLUME 66 *Neil Gaiman and Philosophy: Gods Gone Wild!* (2012) Edited by Tracy L. Bealer, Rachel Luria, and Wayne Yuen

VOLUME 67 *Breaking Bad and Philosophy: Badder Living through Chemistry* (2012) Edited by David R. Koepsell and Robert Arp

VOLUME 68 *The Walking Dead and Philosophy: Zombie Apocalypse Now* (2012) Edited by Wayne Yuen

VOLUME 69 *Curb Your Enthusiasm and Philosophy: Awaken the Social Assassin Within* (2012) Edited by Mark Ralkowski

VOLUME 70 *Dungeons and Dragons and Philosophy: Raiding the Temple of Wisdom* (2012) Edited by Jon Cogburn and Mark Silcox

VOLUME 71 *The Catcher in the Rye and Philosophy: A Book for Bastards, Morons, and Madmen* (2012) Edited by Keith Dromm and Heather Salter

VOLUME 72 *Jeopardy! and Philosophy: What Is Knowledge in the Form of a Question?* (2012) Edited by Shaun P. Young

VOLUME 73 *The Wire and Philosophy: This America, Man* (2013) Edited by David Bzdak, Joanna Crosby, and Seth Vannatta

VOLUME 74 *Planet of the Apes and Philosophy: Great Apes Think Alike* (2013) Edited by John Huss

VOLUME 75 *Psych and Philosophy: Some Dark Juju-Magumbo* (2013) Edited by Robert Arp

VOLUME 76 *The Good Wife and Philosophy: Temptations of Saint Alicia* (2013) Edited by Kimberly Baltzer-Jaray and Robert Arp

VOLUME 77 *Boardwalk Empire and Philosophy: Bootleg This Book* (2013) Edited by Richard Greene and Rachel Robison-Greene

IN PREPARATION:

Frankenstein and Philosophy (2013) Edited by Nicolas Michaud

Futurama and Philosophy (2013) Edited by Courtland Lewis and Shaun P. Young

Ender's Game and Philosophy: Genocide Is Child's Play (2013) Edited by D.E. Wittkower and Lucinda Rush

How I Met Your Mother and Philosophy (2014) Edited by Lorenzo von Matterhorn

Jurassic Park and Philosophy (2014) Edited by Nicolas Michaud

Justified and Philosophy (2014) Edited by Rod Carveth

For full details of all Popular Culture and Philosophy® books, visit www.opencourtbooks.com.

Popular Culture and Philosophy®

Boardwalk Empire and Philosophy

Bootleg This Book

Edited by

RICHARD GREENE

and

RACHEL ROBISON-GREENE

OPEN COURT
Chicago

Volume 77 in the series, Popular Culture and Philosophy®, edited by George A. Reisch

To order books from Open Court, call toll-free 1-800-815-2280, or visit our website at www.opencourtbooks.com.

Open Court Publishing Company is a division of Carus Publishing Company, dba ePals Media.

Copyright © 2013 by Carus Publishing Company, dba ePals Media

First printing 2013

ISBN: 978-0-8126-9832-9

Library of Congress Control Number: 2013942032

For Grant Stevens

Contents

Bottoms Up!   ix

This Is Genuine Stuff   xi

I. Proof Spirits   1

1. Machiavelli on the Boardwalk
   GREG LITTMANN   3

2. Nucky Thompson Superman?
   RICHARD GREENE   25

3. Watching *Boardwalk Empire* with Freud
   RON HIRSCHBEIN   35

4. How to Be Happy on the Boardwalk
   PATRICIA BRACE AND MARIA KINGSBURY   47

II. Medicinal Liqueurs   65

5. Does It Matter that *Boardwalk Empire* Is
   Historically Inaccurate?
   ROD CARVETH   67

6. What's Wrong with Agent Van Alden's God?
   ROBERTO SIRVENT AND NEIL BAKER   79

7. Blaming Nucky Thompson
   MICHAEL DA SILVA   91

8. When It's Right to Lie to a Bootlegger
   DON FALLIS   101

III. Fortified Wines   115

9. Nucky Cleans Up
   WIELAND SCHWANEBECK   117

Contents

10. Absurd Heroes
    RACHEL ROBISON-GREENE   129

11. Fighting for Life in Atlantic City
    JOHN FITZPATRICK   143

IV. From Our Cellars   153

12. The Women of *Boardwalk Empire*
    RACHEL ROBISON-GREENE   155

13. Gillian's Changes
    CHELSI BARNARD ARCHIBALD   165

V. Heady Cocktails   177

14. Two Kinds of Violence in *Boardwalk Empire*
    DEBORAH MELLAMPHY   179

15. The Stories Some People Tell
    CAM COBB   191

The Bootleggers   205

Index   209

Bottoms Up!

Working on this project has been a pleasure, in no small part because of the many fine folks who have assisted us along the way. In particular a debt of gratitude is owed to David Ramsay Steele and George Reisch at Open Court, the writers for this volume, and our respective academic departments at UMass Amherst and Weber State University. Finally, we'd like to thank those family members, students, friends, and colleagues with whom we've had fruitful and rewarding conversations on all things *Boardwalk Empire*.

This Is Genuine Stuff

RICHARD GREENE AND
RACHEL ROBISON-GREENE

From Machiavellian city officials to big-time mobsters (such as Arnold Rothstein, Lucky Luciano, and Al Capone) to corrupt beat cops to overzealous G-men to suffragettes to abolitionists to innocent citizens caught in the crossfire, *Boardwalk Empire* is replete with compelling characters who find themselves in philosophically interesting situations.

As *Boardwalk Empire* is based on historical events and personalities, the philosophical issues raised bear on "real life" in a way that few shows do. We find parallels with the events in *Boardwalk Empire* and contemporary political events, and between the characters in *Boardwalk Empire* (good, bad, and ambiguous) and contemporary figures. *Boardwalk Empire* is one of the most popular cable-TV shows ever, and its popularity is still on the rise.

The tie that binds together the various storylines of *Boardwalk Empire* is Prohibition. The National Prohibition Act of 1919 (aka "The Volstead Act") issued forth an unprecedented rise in organized crime that in many ways we are still recovering from (see modern day Las Vegas and Atlantic City, for example). What's particularly interesting about this boom in crime is the interaction of the various players. For the first time mobsters, gamblers, corrupt politicians (local and national), hillbillies with stills, revolutionary political organizations such Sinn Féin, police officers, g-men on the take, barkeeps, entertainers, prostitutes, and ordinary citizens all sat at the same table with a common enemy—Prohibition! *Boardwalk Empire* beautifully and intensely captures the interplay between these various factions.

It's the story of Nucky Thompson, the Treasurer of Atlantic City during Prohibition, but it's also the story of the Women's Temperance Movement—the movement that helped bring about Prohibition. It's the story of the rise of mob activity in the United States, as well as the story of the often-strained interactions between Italian mobsters, such as Al Capone, Jewish Mobsters, such as Arnold Rothstein, and African American mobsters, such as the fictional Chalky White. It's also a story about the struggle of immigrants in America, and the struggle of women. Finally, it's a story about the aftermath of World War I, and what is was like to return home from the hell of war.

The chapters in this book look at issues in ethics, the history of philosophy, political philosophy, aesthetics, and feminism. Greg Littmann analyzes Nucky Thompson as a Machiavellian Prince. In contrast, Richard Greene casts Thompson in the role of Nietzschean Superman. Chelsi Barnard Archibald provides a Platonic interpretation of *Boardwalk Empire's* most compelling female character—Gillian Darmody. Since every good discussion of Plato deserves an equally good discussion of Aristotle, Pat Brace and Maria Kingsbury discuss Aristotle's notion of happiness as it relates to key characters in *Boardwalk Empire*. Rachel Robison-Greene contributes an existential analysis of Jimmy Darmody and Richard Harrow that focuses on the particular problems that soldiers face upon returning from war. Don Fallis considers the ethics of lying in the seedy world of bootlegging.

Agent Van Alden's unique religious attitudes bring a warped sense of morality to the *Boardwalk* universe. Roberto Sirvent and Neil Baker bring to light the moral character of Van Alden's God. Thompson advises to "never let the truth get in the way of a good story." Rod Carveth explores the role that story telling pays in the series, and Cam Cobb illustrates the role of deception. Wieland Schwanebeck and John Fitzpatrick examine *Boardwalk Empire* through a couple of political lenses: Wieland discusses the body politic, whereas John considers the social contract. Michael Da Silva looks at the difference between causing harms and allowing harms to occur in *Boardwalk Empire*. Deborah Mellamphy considers violence on the boardwalk (spoiler alert: there's no shortage of it). And Ron Hirschbein gives us a compelling Freudian analysis (just when you thought you really knew Jimmy and Gillian!).

So welcome to the Atlantic City of the 1920s. First order of business: pour yourself a couple of stiff drinks (preferably whiskey in crystal dofs). Second order of business: turn to Chapter 1 and start reading. Cheers!

Part I

Proof Spirits

1
Machiavelli on the Boardwalk

GREG LITTMANN

Gentlemen of the Fourth Estate. Tragic though it is, I need hardly remind you that the passage of the Eighteenth Amendment has given rise to a new breed of criminals. Vicious thugs, emboldened by the promise of an easy dollar.

—NUCKY THOMPSON, "A Return to Normalcy"

It should be no surprise that *Boardwalk Empire* is such gripping television. Gangsters fascinate us because power fascinates us. Crime bosses like Enoch "Nucky" Johnson (1888–1968) (Thompson in *Boardwalk Empire*) of Atlantic City, Charles "Lucky" Luciano (1897–1962) of New York, and Alphonse "Scarface Al" Capone (1899–1947) of Chicago continue to intrigue us almost a century after their height of power. Like independent kings, they exercised their authority wherever they could and crushed those who stood in their way.

And why shouldn't such power fascinate us? Whether we like it or not, it's the exercise of power on the grand scale that determines the nature of our lives. Certainly, any political opinions that we hold must be rooted in our interpretation of the ways in which power may be acquired, maintained, and exercised.

Gangsters have often been a source of entertainment, but the study of power and the exercise of power is serious business. Political theorists have scoured history to seek out the principles by which power may be taken and maintained. One of the most famous and influential of these was the Renaissance Italian thinker Niccolò Machiavelli (1469–1527). In his most famous work, *The Prince*, Machiavelli lays out his model for the success of an independent ruler.

Machiavelli's conclusions in *The Prince* have shocked and offended readers for six-hundred years, yet many of them might seem like good sense to Nucky Johnson and other organized criminals of the early twentieth century. Machiavelli believed that if you want to get ahead in the world, or even to stay in power, you have to play dirty. He wrote, "if a prince wants to maintain his rule he must be prepared not to be virtuous, and to make use of this or not according to need."[1]

Previous treatises on government had urged rulers to be just and honest, but Machiavelli said that "some of the things that appear to be virtues will, if he practices them, ruin him, and some of the things that appear to be vices will bring him security and prosperity" (p. 51). As if he were describing Nucky, Machiavelli wrote, "Princes who have achieved great things have been those who have given their word lightly, who have known how to trick men with their cunning, and who, in the end, have overcome those abiding by honest principles" (p. 56). In the first episode of *Boardwalk Empire*, (also given the episode title "Boardwalk Empire"), Nucky Thompson tells Jimmy Darmody, "First rule of politics, kiddo: Never let the truth get in the way of a good story."

Asking how Machiavelli might advise the crime bosses featured on *Boardwalk Empire*, and whether the lives of the crime bosses bear out his principles, is not just an intellectual game. How plausible political theories are depends on how well they stack up against the historical record. Machiavelli himself illustrated his rules of power with examples drawn from recent Italian history and the ancient world. As Machiavelli says: "The prince must read history, studying the

---

[1] Niccolò Machiavelli, *The Prince* (London: Penguin, 2011), p. 50.

actions of eminent men to see how they conducted themselves during war and to discover the reasons for their victories or their defeats, so that he can avoid the latter and imitate the former" (p. 49). He never commented directly on the bosses of organized criminal syndicates, but that's no reason not to examine how applicable his recommendations are to independent rulers of all descriptions.

Machiavelli's task in writing *The Prince* was not to describe government as it should ideally operate. Rather, his interest was in describing which techniques actually *work* as tools of political power for independent rulers and for those who wish to become independent princes by legitimate or criminal means. Similarly, when I discuss the strategies employed by various crime bosses and compare their effectiveness, I'm not suggesting that the most effective strategies are thereby morally acceptable. None of the successful crime bosses of the era acted in a morally acceptable manner, and I hope that you will join me in taking a moment to raise a sincere middle finger to all criminals, past and present, who have used corruption, theft, and violence to feed their greed at the expense of the people around them. That accomplished, what are the rules of power?

Winners Seize Opportunities

GASTON MEANS: Consider me an admirer, Mr. Thompson. Ordinary men avoid trouble. Extraordinary men turn it to their advantage. You and I have that in common.

—"Spaghetti and Coffee"

Machiavelli stressed the need for a ruler to constantly modernize their approach, changing and adapting to suit the environment. He wrote: "The one who adapts his policy to the times prospers, and likewise . . . the one whose policy clashes with the demands of the times does not" (p. 80). Machiavelli would approve of the way that Nucky Johnson grabbed the business opportunity offered by the ratification of the Eighteenth Amendment in 1919, prohibiting "the manufacture, sale, or transportation of intoxicating liquors within, the importation thereof into, or the exportation thereof from the United States and all territory . . ." Nucky recognized the enormous advantage that freely flowing booze would give to the tourist industry in Atlantic City and worked to ensure that nothing would interfere with supply.

Thanks to Nucky, Prohibition just meant that Atlantic City would dub itself "The World's Playground." Machiavelli would likewise approve of the initiative shown by young criminals like Arnold "The Brain" Rothstein (1882–1928), Johnny "The Fox" Torrio (1882–1957), Al Capone, Lucky Luciano, and Meyer Lansky (1902–1983) in making money from the new source of bootleg alcohol.

Being overly cautious in exploiting new opportunities is positively dangerous in Machiavelli's view. He wrote: "A man who is circumspect, when circumstances demand impetuous behavior, is unequal to the task, and so he comes to grief" (p. 80). Nothing illustrates this more clearly than the fate of James "Diamond Jim" Colosimo (1878–1920), the Chicago crime boss who failed to capitalize on Prohibition and paid with his life, as dramatized in the *Boardwalk Empire* pilot episode.

Colosimo declined to involve his organization in booze, fearing the police attention that it might attract. He was already very rich from prostitution, gambling, and racketeering, and saw no need to change a winning formula. This limited the ability of men working under him to make money. Johnny Torrio, Colosimo's nephew and second in command, decided to murder him and take over his operation. Torrio arranged to meet Diamond Jim at his restaurant, Colosimo's Café, but when the boss arrived, he was gunned down in the doorway by an unknown assailant before he could even draw the pearl-handled .38 he kept in his pocket.

Machiavelli's principles that power requires change and that failure to seize new opportunities is positively dangerous are similarly borne out by the revolution of modernization headed by Lucky Luciano in New York. The two biggest New York bosses, Gieuseppe "Joe the Boss" Masseria (1886–1931) and Salvatore Maranzano (1886–1931), were old-fashioned in their business practices. Particularly limiting was their re-luctance to work with non-Italians, or even non-Sicilians. Their failure to exploit the business opportunity offered by co-operation with criminals of other ethnicities, especially the Irish and Jewish organizations, meant less profit for the younger gangsters working under them, who resented the restrictions imposed by the conservative "mustache Petes." Luciano saw an opportunity to take over.

Having earned enough respect to become a trusted lieu-tenant of Masseria, Luciano arranged his murder on behalf of the rival crime boss Maranzano. He invited Masseria to a sit-down at Nuova Villa Tammaro in Coney Island, and while Joe the Boss was enjoying a good meal, four of Luciano's as-sociates entered the restaurant and shot him from behind, planting four bullets in his back and one in his head. Having become Maranzano's second in command, Luciano had Maranzano killed too. Four assassins on loan from Meyer Lansky dropped by Maranzano's Park Avenue office pretend-ing to be police officers and shot and stabbed him to death. The "Luciano family" was Lucky's unified organization com-bined of the Masseria and Maranzano factions. Working with other bosses, Luciano would go on to reorganize and modern-ize the American Mafia to maximize profits.

Machiavelli believed that the danger posed by not tak-ing action to exploit changing circumstances is much greater than the danger posed by being too rash. He wrote, "it is better to be impetuous than circumspect" (p. 81). This may seem strange given the great dangers involved in open conflict, but Machiavelli believed that "there is no avoiding war; it can only be postponed to the advantage of others" (p. 12). In other words, you have to hurry to deal with your rivals before they manage to deal with you. Machiavelli held up the success of the aggressively expansionistic Roman Empire as his model, observing that the Romans were never "tempted to make the most of the present time; rather, they made the most of their own prowess and pru-dence" (p. 12). Machiavelli would respect the unbridled am-bition of a Nucky Johnson or a Lucky Luciano.

It may seem surprising that the organizations of Colosimo, Masseria, and Maranzano were taken over with such little resistance once the old boss was dead, just as it may seem surprising that the Commodore's organization was taken over by Nucky Johnson with little resistance when the Commodore was sent to prison in 1913 (which happened in reality, as on *Boardwalk Empire*). However, Machiavelli would not be surprised: "men willingly change their ruler, expecting to fare better" (p. 8). Even when the change is forced on them, they're unlikely to object very strenuously if the change doesn't put them under any hardship: "Men are won over by the present far more than by the past; and when they decide that what is being done here and now is good, they content themselves with that" (p. 77). He believed that people are primarily concerned with whether they are allowed to carry on with their business and maintain their way of life: "So long as their old ways of life are undisturbed and there is no divergence in customs, men live quietly" (p. 9).

Luciano, taking Meyer Lansky's advice, paid particular attention to the maintenance of customs as a stabilizing factor. Even as he reorganized and modernized the Cosa Nostra, he kept in place the old mafia rituals, such as all that theatrical silliness involving drops of blood and the burning images of saints when a new recruit joins the organization and becomes a "man of honor." The need not to interfere with customs applies just as much to the customs of society in general. For all the criminal deeds undertaken by Arnold Rothstein, the one for which he received the most negative attention was allegedly fixing the 1919 World Series. Americans will tolerate organized crime up to a point, but not when it interferes with *baseball*.

Murder as a Tool of Business

NUCKY THOMPSON: How's Torrio handling the competition?

AL CAPONE: We're killing them.

—"A Dangerous Maid"

Machiavelli would even approve of how willing so many gangsters of the period were to kill their rivals. He believed that it was dangerous to do harm to someone (which would include harming their business) but let that person live. He wrote, "Men must be either pampered or crushed, because they can get revenge for small injuries but not for grievous ones. So any injury a prince does to a man should be of such a kind that there is no fear of revenge" (pp. 10–11).

In the television series *Boardwalk Empire*, the damage done to gangsters by those they have harmed but not killed drives much of the plot. Most obviously, Nucky Thompson brings a lot of trouble on himself by waiting until the end of Season Two to do what he has been threatening to do since the second episode of the show, and murder his protégé, the fictional gangster James "Jimmy" Darmody. Nucky harms Jimmy in "The Ivory Tower" when he fires him and makes him pay three thousand dollars for hijacking Arnold Rothstein's liquor shipment without permission, and harms him again in "Broadway Limited" when he forces him to leave Atlantic City. Nucky's leniency comes back to haunt him as Jimmy plots to replace Nucky as boss of Atlantic City and eventually, in "Peg of Old," orders Nucky's murder.

Darmody himself suffers because he fails to heed Machiavelli's warning against harming rivals without killing them. If he had executed all of Rothstein's men when he hijacked the shipment, a survivor would not have identified him to agent Van Alden in "Broadway Limited." Likewise, if Darmody had killed the Chicago crime boss Charlie Sheridan instead of just muscling into his territory, Sheridan would never have mutilated Darmody's love interest, the prostitute Pearl, in "Anastasia." Conversely, if Sheridan had killed Darmody instead of just mutilating Pearl, Darmody would not have finally shot and killed him in "Home."

More significantly, crime bosses have followed Machiavelli's principle in real life, even if they never read Machiavelli. The war between Masseria and Maranzano in New York dragged on for years, with many deaths but without either boss striking a decisive blow. When Lucky Luciano had

Masseria assassinated in 1931, he put an end to the war, because Masseria could not retaliate. Likewise, when Luciano had Maranzano assassinated later that same year, he was able to take over his organization smoothly, because Maranzano was out of the picture. If Maranzano had taken Machiavelli's advice, he never would have let Luciano live long enough to betray him. After all, Luciano had plenty of reason to want revenge.

In a textbook example of harming a person without crushing them, Maranzano's men abducted Luciano in 1929, while he was working for Masseria. They stabbed him and beat him so badly that he gained his trademark facial scar and droopy eyelid, but he was still alive when they dumped him onto the beach on Long Island. Was it an incompetent murder attempt or was a decision made to spare Luciano's life? Either way, his permanent disfigurement and near death as a result of Maranzano's orders can't have encouraged Luciano to feel loyalty to his new boss when Maranzano made him second in command.

Why did Maranzano trust a man to whom he had done such visible harm? Presumably, he thought that Luciano cared only about making money, and perhaps he was even right about that. All the same, as Machiavelli notes, "Whoever believes that with great men new services wipe out old injuries deceives himself" (p. 28). To Luciano's mind, the importance of crushing the one you harm extends even to old friends like Benjamin "Bugsy" Siegel (1906–1947) ("Benny Siegel" in *Boardwalk Empire*). When Siegel invested six million dollars of the mob's money in his Flamingo Hotel in the little nowhere-town of Las Vegas, and was showing no sign of ever being able to pay it back, Luciano has him killed rather than simply taking over the operation. He wasn't about to take away the dream of a man like Bugsy (that is, "crazy as a bed-bug") Siegel, and leave him around to take revenge.

The degree of blood-letting that a ruler should engage in, according to Machiavelli, will depend on his situation. Some rulers have more people in the way of their ambitions than others. In particular, a ruler is more likely to benefit from drastic measures if they are ruling a newly conquered kingdom than if they are taking over from the old ruler as a matter of orderly succession. Machiavelli wrote: "A new prince, of all rulers, finds it impossible to avoid a reputation for cruelty, because of the abundant dangers inherent in a newly won state" (p. 54). After all, "governments set up overnight, like everything in nature whose growth is forced, lack strong roots" (pp. 22–23). On the other hand "in hereditary states, accustomed to their prince's family, there are far fewer difficulties in maintaining one's rule" (p. 7).

When Nucky Johnson became boss of the corrupt Atlantic City Republican organization, he was taking over a very well-established institution in accordance with established (if unofficial) procedures. Nucky was not born to be a crime boss, but he *was* born as an insider to the political machine that he would eventually inherit. Nucky's father, the crooked sheriff Smith Johnson (1853–1917), was a friend and loyal retainer to boss Louis "the Commodore" Kuehnle (1857–1934), represented by the character Louis "the Commodore" Kaestner in *Boardwalk Empire*.

Kuehnle was head of the society that controlled Atlantic City politics, milking businesses and government employees for kickbacks and allowing gambling and prostitution to flourish in return for protection money. Nucky became his father's undersheriff at the age of twenty-one and rose quickly through the ranks of Kuehnle's organization. He was so well-respected by thirty that he was the obvious person to take over as boss when state governor Woodrow Wilson sent the Commodore to prison in 1913 for profiting from government contracts. Kuehnle didn't hand over power willingly, but his machine passed smoothly into Nucky's hands without the need for reorganization or the replacement of officials.

It was business as usual in Atlantic City. For other crime bosses, seizing and holding power was more difficult. The juvenile street gangs of New York's Lower East Side were the training ground for Johnny Torrio, Al Capone, Lucky Luciano, Meyer Lansky, and Bugsy Siegel. They had to claw their way to power and fight hard to keep it. It is perhaps not surprising, then, that gangsters like these tended to shed more blood than Nucky Johnson.

Gangland Warfare

THE COMMODORE: When you come face to face with destiny, do you want to be the bear? Or do you want to be the one holding the shotgun?

—"Ourselves Alone"

Most crime bosses, like most historical kings, have to be able to look to their own defense, there being no higher authority to call on for help. Such independent leaders have to ask themselves how much of their time and resources should be devoted to warfare. Machiavelli was unequivocal:

A prince . . . must have no other object or thought, nor acquire skill in anything, except war, its organization, and its discipline. The art of war . . . is so useful that besides enabling hereditary princes to maintain their rule it frequently enables ordinary citizens to become rulers. (p. 47)

Machiavelli would praise Nucky Johnson for achieving a position in which he had effective command over so many troops. With the police of Atlantic City firmly under his control, Nucky had an impressive local monopoly on force. On the other hand, Machiavelli would probably criticize Nucky for neglecting the use of force as a tool for actively crushing his enemies. Nucky's tools of choice were money and political influence. He was a businessman, not a general, and was much less interested in killing his rivals than he was in raking in the profits of his corruption. Machiavelli might be more approving of the attitude shown by Al Capone, who was always eager to solve his problems with violence. Most dramatically, Capone spent four of his six years as head of the Chicago Outfit in a war for Chicago against the equally aggressive North Side Gang under Earl "Hymie" Weis, Vincent "The Schemer" Drucci and George "Bugs" Moran. The occasional truce to recover strength aside, each of the two criminal organizations were dedicated to wiping the other out by force, resulting in the murder of five hundred people or more.

Obviously, living this way requires alertness, cunning, and nerves of steel. Machiavelli wrote that a ruler "must learn from the fox and the lion; because the lion is defenseless against traps and a fox is defenseless against wolves. Therefore one must be a fox in order to recognize traps, and a lion to frighten off wolves" (p. 56). Johnny "The Fox" Torrio, who had been boss of the Chicago Outfit before Capone, earned his nickname "The Fox" because of his cunning, but his nerves failed him in the end. It was Torrio who began the war between the Chicago Outfit and the North Side Gang in 1924 when he had the North Side boss Dion O'Banion gunned down in the back room of his florist's shop. But when the North Side Gang returned the gesture by shooting up Torrio's car, it was more than he could take. Hymie Weis and Bugs Moran personally opened up on his limousine with a .45 automatic and a .12 gauge shotgun, hitting him five times and almost killing him. Johnny "The Fox" Torrio retired to Brooklyn and handed the Chicago outfit over to the lion Capone.

Machiavelli believed that security lies in having a strong military. A ruler's "defense lies in being well armed and having good allies; and if he is well armed he will always have good allies" (p. 59). That having force at your disposal brings you allies is evidenced by the way that men like Nucky, Luciano, and Capone found allies in one another, bearing no good will to each other, but bound by a mutual recognition of each other's strength and usefulness. It is further evidenced by Luciano's ability in 1931 to unite the Cosa Nostra under a new regulatory body, the Commission. Criminal "families" who had nothing but long-standing hatred for one another were willing to take one another as allies out of a recognition of what could be done with their mutual strength.

On the other hand, Machiavelli believed that a ruler without military strength won't have any friends to help them either. "You are bound to meet misfortune if you are unarmed because, among other reasons, people despise you" (p. 48). It goes without saying that in the world of organized crime, a criminal who is not protected by others and cannot meet force with force will quickly be pushed aside by stronger rivals. This is something that many of the most successful criminal bosses of prohibition learned as children in street gangs, shaking down pushcart merchants or running dice games to cheat other kids. Machiavelli believed that it was impossible to resolve civil problems without military superiority, while once you have military superiority, civil problems will work themselves out: "The main foundations of every state . . . are good laws and good arms . . . you cannot have good laws without good arms, and where there are good arms, good laws inevitably follow" (p. 40).

The Need for Respectability

> NUCKY THOMPSON: You wanna be taken seriously? Then learn how to fuckin' speak!
>
> —"Nights in Ballygran"

Machiavelli understood as well as any successful crime boss how vital appearances are to the exercise of power. A prince, like a crime boss, has influence in proportion to his reputation—to have power is to be able to convince people that it would be sensible to do what you tell them to. Further, like successful bosses, Machiavelli understood that the image you present has to be tailored to the specific audience you're trying to impress. He believed that soldiers respect brutality in their leaders, writing "when a prince is campaigning with his soldiers . . . he need not worry about having a reputation for cruelty; because, without such a reputation, no army was ever kept united and disciplined" (p. 55). He might therefore counsel crime bosses to cultivate an image of aggression and brutality among fellow gangsters. He might approve, for instance, of the way that Al Capone so famously and dramatically dealt with the disloyalty of Albert Anselmi and John

Scalise in 1929 by inviting them to a lavish banquet at an Indiana roadhouse and concluding the feast by beating them with a baseball bat and having them shot. Capone wasn't simply getting Anselmi and Scalise out of the way. He was sending a message to the other guests about what sort of man he was.

Far from condemning Capone for dispatching his enemies in a dishonorable way, Machiavelli would praise the gangster's cunning. Machiavelli holds up a similar fatal banquet as a model of intelligent ambition. He describes how Oliverotto of Fermo betrayed his uncle Giovanni Fogliani, to whom he owed his position and fortune, by holding a formal banquet for Fogliani and the other leading citizens of Fermo, at which the guests were slaughtered in a surprise attack by Oliverotto's men. Capone could hardly have followed Oliverotto's example more closely without taking a baseball bat to his old friend Johnny Torrio. Torrio himself, of course, had murdered his uncle and patron, Diamond Jim Colosimo, to take over Colosimo's organization. Some traditions, it seems, never change.

A vicious image is counter-productive with the public, however, as both Machiavelli and successful crime bosses have understood. A criminal's freedom to operate can be no greater than what the public is willing to tolerate. Not even a king (let alone a crime boss) can withstand the united will of the people. As Machiavelli said, "a prince can never make himself safe against a hostile people; there are too many of them" (p. 33). Fortunately for princes and gangsters, "everyone sees what you appear to be, few experience what you really are" (p. 58). He wrote: "The common people are always impressed by appearances and results." As far as appearances go, the ruler should cultivate a public image of someone who is "compassionate, faithful to his word, kind, guileless, and devout" (p. 57) and is "a man of good faith, a man of integrity, a kind and religious man" (p. 58). On the other hand, "He will be despised if he has a reputation for being fickle, frivolous, effeminate, cowardly, irresolute; a prince should . . . strive to demonstrate in his actions grandeur, courage, sobriety, strength" (p. 59).

Nucky Johnson was a master at passing himself off as an honest and upright citizen. He served as secretary to the Republican County Committee, county treasurer, and even clerk of the New Jersey State Supreme Court. Always elegantly dressed (he had more than a hundred hand-tailored suits) and with his trademark red carnation in his lapel, he participated in meetings of the Fourth Ward Republican Club and hosted and attended lavish society parties. Nelson Johnson, in his riveting non-fiction book *Boardwalk Empire*, upon which the television series is based, relates that on the night of the largest meeting of prohibitionist reformers ever held in Atlantic City, Nucky "was at the Ritz Carlton entertaining the governor, his cabinet, and the entire state legislature, Republican and Democrat alike."[2]

In the case of other bosses, learning to project the right public appearance was an essential part of the transformation from street thug to businessman. In the series *Boardwalk Empire*, we see Arnold Rothstein in the process of civilizing Lucky Luciano and Meyer Lansky. Luciano said of Rothstein "He taught me how to dress. . . . how to use knives and forks and things like that at the dinner table, about holding a door open for a girl."[3] Likewise, Johnny Torrio was taught how to dress, speak, and present himself by Paul Kelly, leader of the Five Points Gang, while Torrio in his turn would act as mentor for Al Capone. In time, Capone would lose his Brooklyn accent and begin to make appearances at the opera and other society events, playing the part of a respectable entrepreneur.

---

[2] Nelson Johnson, *Boardwalk Empire* (London: Ebury, 2011), p, 98

[3] David Pietrusza, *Rothstein: The Life, Times, and Murder of the Criminal Genius Who Fixed the 1919 World Series* (New York: Basic Books, 2011), p. 201.

Keeping the People Happy

ELI THOMPSON: Nobody cares about you. They just care about what you can give them.

—"Paris Green"

The American gangsters of the early twentieth century could even teach Machiavelli a thing or two about the art of propaganda. For instance, some of them understood much better than he did how useful a reputation for *generosity* could be as a tool for political power. Machiavelli declared it useless to seek such a reputation, writing "If you want to sustain a reputation for generosity . . . you have to be ostentatiously lavish; and a prince acting in that fashion will soon squander all his resources" (p. 51). American organized criminals have proved him wrong.

While in real terms, Nucky Johnson may have had his hand in the pockets of the ordinary citizens of Atlantic City, he successfully cultivated a reputation for generosity by flamboyantly giving back a fraction of what he took. He was an ostentatious supporter of charity and often sought opportunities to help individuals in need. In the pilot episode of *Boardwalk Empire*, Nucky Thompson meets Margaret Schroder, a pregnant member of the Temperance League with an unemployed husband, and insists on giving her money.

While the event is fictional, the act is representative of Nucky Johnson's attitude. Dropping tips of a hundred dollars or more in nightclubs and restaurants, he would also hand out dollar bills to the poor as a matter of routine as he took his daily stroll on the boardwalk, taking particular care to single out children to pat on the head and hand a buck or two. Nucky was especially careful to help members of Atlantic City's black population, who were hardest hit by tough economic times. His generosity worked: black voters traditionally turned out for Nucky.

Al Capone was also particularly successful in winning a reputation for generosity. An active supporter of charities, he wanted to be seen as a modern-day Robin Hood, a law-breaker but a friend of the poor. When the depression struck, Capone opened the first soup kitchen for the unemployed in Chicago, feeding up to five thousand people a night.

You'll recall that along with appearances, the other thing that Machiavelli said the common people are impressed by is results. During the prohibition era, one result that the public cared an awful lot about was whether the alcohol kept flowing. The hotel business in Atlantic City was flourishing because Nucky Johnson and his organization made sure that out-of-towners could get a drink, while respectable but thirsty people in Chicago and New York were satisfied thanks to the efforts of men like Torrio, Capone, Rothstein, Lansky and Luciano. Machiavelli wrote: "Wise princes have always taken great pains . . . to satisfy the people and keep them content" (p. 61). As Nelson Johnson notes in his book *Boardwalk Empire*, Nucky Johnson once said, "We have whiskey, wine, women, song, and slot machines. I won't deny it and I won't apologize for it. If the majority of the people didn't want them, they wouldn't be profitable and wouldn't exist," (*Boardwalk Empire*, p. 87) while Al Capone famously observed, "I make my money by supplying a public demand. . . . Everybody calls me a racketeer. I call myself a business-man. When I sell liquor, it's bootlegging. When my patrons serve it on a silver tray on Lake Shore Drive, it's hospitality" (p. 86). Breaking the rules becomes a strength when the people want to break the rules too. Machiavelli wrote: "because whenever that class of men on which you believe your continued rule depends is corrupt, whether it be the populace, or soldiers, or nobles, you have to satisfy it by adopting the same disposition" (p. 63).

The Danger of Being Hated

ARNOLD ROTHSTEIN: Reputation takes a lifetime to build, but only seconds to destroy.

—"Belle Femme"

Machiavelli recognized that not every ruler could both maintain power and enjoy a sterling reputation for virtue. However, he also recognized the vital importance of not incurring hatred. Dirty tricks may be all very useful, but a ruler who goes too far becomes despised and a ruler who becomes despised is in danger. Machiavelli wrote:

> So a prince has of necessity to be so prudent that he knows how to escape the evil reputation attached to those vices which could lose him his state. (p. 51)

Once again, the history of American gangsters in the early twentieth century bears out Machiavelli's principle. As effective as so many American gangsters were in cultivating public opinion, a failure to maintain an appropriate public image has been the downfall of many of the most famous. Even if having a public image problem is an intrinsic part of working in organized crime, that only makes it all the more important to avoid unnecessary resentment.

For Nucky Johnson, it was not enough to *be* incredibly wealthy; everyone had to *know* that he was incredibly wealthy. Renting the entire ninth floor of the luxury Ritz Carlton Hotel as his home, the so called "Czar of the Ritz" threw lavish parties for hundreds of guests, throwing around money far in excess of his meager legal income. When he went out on business, it was in his chauffeur-driven, powder-blue Rolls Royce limousine (if not in one of his four other cars). He purchased whole blocks of World Series tickets for his friends, and on more than one occasion, flew the entire cast of a Broadway play to Atlantic City for a weekend at his expense.

For as long as Nucky's reign brought prosperity to the city, his ostentatious lifestyle brought him celebrity. However, the public attitude grew colder as Atlantic City was hit with the double economic disasters of the great depression and the repeal of prohibition. Nucky was targeted for criticism by the newspaper mogul William Randolph Hearst and the Roosevelt administration found it politically worthwhile to send IRS and FBI agents, like the fictional Nelson Van Alden in *Boardwalk Empire*, to begin undercover investigations in Atlantic City, eventually leading to Nucky's imprisonment and decline as a crime boss.

Machiavelli wrote of the hereditary prince that "if he does not provoke hatred with extraordinary vices . . . his subjects should naturally be well disposed towards him" (p. 8). Perhaps if Nucky had not celebrated his wealth so openly, it would not have been so obvious that his wealth so vastly exceeded his legitimate income. Perhaps if he had not flouted the law so flagrantly, or so visibly enjoyed a life of luxury and excess at a time when other Americans were suffering so badly, then there wouldn't have been enough political capital in bringing him to justice to make him a target of the FBI and IRS.

Lucky Luciano could likewise have benefitted from following Machiavelli's advice and trying to avoid contempt. Like Nucky, Luciano loved being rich and (against the advice of Meyer Lansky as well as Machiavelli), loved to flaunt his wealth. He even, like Nucky, rented the entire floor of a luxury hotel as his home, working out of the *Waldorf Towers*. He frequented the coolest New York nightclubs, joints like the Copacabana and the 21 Club. He loved to rub shoulders with the famous, loved to be recognized, and basked in his celebrity. One of the questions that Luciano was unable to answer on the witness stand prior to being sent to prison in 1936 was how he could live such a lavish lifestyle on a reported income of $22,000 per year. Perhaps if he had not been so keen to advertise who he was and what he got away with, he might not have been targeted by special prosecutor Thomas E. Dewey and might not have been sentenced to thirty to fifty years.

Al Capone, like Nucky and Luciano, might have profited from heeding Machiavelli and avoiding unnecessary hatred. However, like Nucky and Luciano, Capone loved to advertise his wealth and success. He bought himself a luxury mansion on Palm Island, Florida, and his diamond pinky ring alone cost a purported $50,000. Even to be envied was not enough; Capone wanted the public to love him, and his need for attention eventually made him the most famous gangster in the world. His fierce protection of his image was counterproductive. When accused of crimes, he would call a press conference, intending to defend himself but in effect calling attention to the accusations, which were, after all, true.

In 1926, Capone faced trial for his gang's accidental slaying of Assistant State's Attorney William McSwiggan with stray Thompson gun bullets while firing on another gang. He was acquitted because he paid officials and terrified witnesses, but a wiser man would have laid low for a while. Instead, Capone soon took the theatrical step of presenting himself at a courthouse, a jail and a police station, with a reporter in tow, asking if he was wanted on any charges, just so that the authorities would have to tell him he wasn't. While Capone succeeded in becoming something of a folk hero, someone who earns a living by illegal means can't afford such exposure.

Al Capone's public perception was increasingly damaged by the rising death toll of his war with the North Side Gang, culminating in the infamous St. Valentine's Day Massacre of 1929 in which Capone's men staged a fake police raid, lined seven captive members of the rival organization against a wall, and gunned them down with submachine guns, shotguns, and a revolver. The violence was becoming too much for the public to romanticize. The editorial in the Chicago *Tribune* on February 14th announced:

> The murders went out of the comprehension of a civilized city. . . . The butchering of seven men by open daylight raises this question for Chicago: Is it helpless?

Machiavelli advises the prince to be bold and ruthless in wiping out enemies, but Machiavelli has no sympathy for those, like Capone, who over-reach themselves and bring about their own downfall though unchecked ambition. He wrote: "The wish to acquire more is admittedly a very natural and common thing; and when men succeed in this they are always praised rather than condemned. But when they lack the ability to do so and yet want to acquire more at all costs, they deserve condemnation for their mistakes" (p. 14). Perhaps, if Capone had not tried to be a celebrity and had not been so brazen in his violence that he inspired public hatred, he might not have been targeted by President Herbert Hoover and might not have ended up in Alcatraz.

Capone once admitted, "It is upon fear . . . that I have built up my organization,"[4] and Machiavelli would have no objection to that per se. Machiavelli thought that a ruler *must* be feared in order to be secure. In fact, he came to the grim conclusion that "it is far better to be feared than loved if you cannot be both. One can make this generalization about men: they are ungrateful, fickle, liars, and deceivers, they shun danger and are greedy for profit. . . . Men worry less about doing an injury to one who makes himself loved than to one who makes himself feared. For love is secured by a bond of gratitude which men, wretched creatures that they are, break when it is to their advantage to do so; but fear is strengthened by a dread of punishment which is always effective." However, "The prince must none the less make himself feared in such a way that, if he is not loved, at least he escapes being hated" (p. 54). While a ruler who has too little brutality has no security, according to Machiavelli, a ruler who has too *much* brutality will have no security either, because beyond a certain point, brutality feeds opposition rather than suppressing it.

Lessons from the Boardwalk

NUCKY THOMPSON: The beginning's over. The end hasn't come yet. All I care about is now.

—"Under God's Power She Flourishes"

That's my take on what Machiavelli would say about Nucky Johnson and other major crime bosses featured on *Board-*

---

[4] Cornelius Vanderbilt, Jr., "How Al Capone Would Run This Country," *Liberty* (October 17th, 1931).

walk Empire, where Machiavelli's advice might have helped the bosses, and where the crime bosses had insights into power that eluded Machiavelli. But what does looking at the bosses through Machiavelli's eyes teach us about *power?* I think that the history of organized crime in the US in the first half of the twentieth century, along with human history in general, backs up much of what Machiavelli says in *The Prince*.

It would be nice to be able to deny that liars have gotten ahead in the world, but we know that they often have, and individuals like Nucky Johnson, Lucky Luciano, and Al Capone provide examples of just how far some liars have gotten. The exploits of criminals like these back up Machiavelli's claims that appearances are central to political power, that maintaining power requires change and the exploitation of new opportunities as they arise, and that security requires military force. I think that history even shows Machiavelli to be right that it is dangerous to harm people without killing them, although I also think that the lesson of history is that we should strive not to harm people rather than that we should kill them on little provocation.

Machiavelli says that from the point of view of maintaining power, it is best to be both loved and feared, but that if you can't be both, it's better to be feared than loved. He's right about the importance of fear insofar as a ruler or people are in danger if potential enemies don't take their defenses seriously. However, Machiavelli also said that it's vital not to be hated, and I think that this is his most important observation. Nucky Johnson, Lucky Luciano, Al Capone, Arnold Rothstein, and Johnny Torrio were all removed from power by hatred that they had inspired against themselves. Perhaps a crime boss cannot avoid being hated, but even so, the more hated a ruler becomes, the less secure that ruler's power.

Nothing illustrates this more clearly than a pair of stories about Arnold Rothstein, one from *Boardwalk Empire* and one from real life. In the *Boardwalk Empire* pilot, Rothstein travels to Atlantic City to do business with Nucky Thompson and other bosses, then decides to cheat in Nucky's casino while he's there, just because he can get away with it. Rothstein doesn't need the money, and besides, his financial interests are best served by smooth co-operation with Nucky. Yet Rothstein harms himself by sabotaging his relationship with Nucky through arrogance and the need to flaunt his power.

The event is fictional, but is in the spirit of the real man. In 1928, at the age of forty-six, Arnold Rothstein staggered into the Park Central Hotel with a gunshot wound to his abdomen. As he lay dying, he refused to identify his assassin, advising the police, "You stick to your trade. I'll stick to mine,"[6] but it is generally believed that he was shot for refusing to pay his gambling debt to George "Hump" McManus. How can it be that a man as cunning and successful as Arnold Rothstein—"Mr. Big," "The Brain," "The Big Bankroll," "The Man Uptown"—could throw away everything he worked for by welshing on debts that it was well within his ability to pay? He didn't know he was going to be shot, of course, but even if you love gambling, it's foolish to gamble with your life. It seems that Mr. Big grew too proud and threw his weight around too freely. He could have lived to old age in luxury, but because he made himself unnecessarily hated, he was destroyed.

As voters in first world democracies, we are all co-rulers with the responsibility to decide on government policy. History has shown again and again the downfall of those rulers who made themselves unnecessarily hated. Let us hope that we and our fellow voters have the sense to treat the citizens of other nations in a way that will avoid unnecessary hatred, if only for our own sakes.

---

[6] Selwyn Rabb, *Five Families: The Rise, Decline, and Resurgence of America's Most Powerful Mafia Empires* (New York: St. Martin's Press, 2006), p. 40.

2
Nucky Thompson Superman?

RICHARD GREENE

> *I teach you the Superman*. Man is something that is to be surpassed. What have ye done to surpass man?
>
> —FRIEDRICH NIETZSCHE, *Thus Spake Zarathustra*

The great philosopher Friedrich Nietzsche, in *Thus Spake Zarathustra*, wrote of the Übermensch or the Superman. The Übermensch is the successor to God in a world where "God is dead," and is the teacher of the eternal recurrence. So what exactly does this mean? Well, let's get started on the question: Is Nucky Thompson Nietzsche's Superman?

Why the Superman? Surely there must be a better fit somewhere in the history of philosophy for Nucky Thompson than comparing him to Nietzsche's vision of the ideal human and goal for all humanity! Nucky Thompson, charming as he can be at times, is a murderer, a mobster, a con man, a philanderer, a corrupt politician, a bootlegger, a lousy brother, a hot-head, and a not so pleasant guy to work for.

Why not compare him to the incorrigible fellows that Plato describes in Book II of *The Republic*? One has a reputation for being perfectly just and uses that reputation to be perfectly unjust, and the other is a shepherd who uses an invisible ring to take over a kingdom by raping the queen and murdering the king? Or why not compare him (as Greg Littmann does in the previous chapter) to Machiavelli's

Prince—the cunning ruler who learned to keep his friends close and his enemies closer.

Perhaps we'd be better off comparing Nucky to Hobbes's mighty Leviathan, or Dostoevsky's Underground Man (not the easiest guy to get along with) or Descartes's Evil Genius (speaking very metaphorically, of course). Each of these seems apt in some ways. In fact, the comparison with Machiavelli's Prince seems even more apt. Nucky Thompson can be seen as a study in Machiavellian political theory. And yet, there are aspects of Nucky Thompson's character or psychological make-up or personality that these other comparisons just don't quite capture. Moreover, not despite, but in virtue of Nucky's aforementioned shortcomings, he is well on his way to becoming Nietzsche's Superman.

God Is Dead! What Do We Do Now?

Nietzsche's Übermensch has it origins in his book *The Gay Science*. A madman (who turns out to be not so mad) runs into town exclaiming that "God is Dead!" For Nietzsche this means two things, neither of which is that God has literally died:

1. people no longer believe in God,

and

2. the story of God no longer fulfills the purpose it once did (which is to reinforce Christian morality, or as Nietzsche puts it "slave morality").

The madman continues his rant:

How shall we comfort ourselves, the murderers of all murderers? What was holiest and mightiest of all that the world has yet owned has bled to death under our knives: who will wipe this blood off us? What water is there for us to clean ourselves? What festivals of atonement, what sacred games shall we have to invent? Is not the greatness of this deed too great for us? Must we ourselves not become gods simply to appear worthy of it? There has never been a greater deed; and whoever is born after us—for the sake of this deed he will belong to a higher history than all history hitherto.[1]

So, for Nietzsche, God needs to be replaced, and another God won't do the trick. This is where the Übermensch comes in. The Übermensch is man, but not just any man; it is man overcoming himself of all illness that the now dead God of Christianity has bestowed upon him. Nietzsche says that man is a rope, tied between beast and Übermensch, and that man is something to be overcome. So, in a sense, the Übermensch can be thought of as a next step in man's evolution, not in our physical evolution, but in our moral and psychological evolution. While Nietzsche values our animal natures, he doesn't want to return to them.

Man must move forward. Can Nucky Thompson be the next step? Is Nucky Thompson really God's successor? Is Nucky Thompson (to use Nietzsche's way of putting things) going to achieve in himself what nations once achieved? We'll see.

What Rough Beast Is This Übermensch?

To determine whether Nucky Thompson is a good candidate for the Übermensch, we'll need to get a better idea of what Nietzsche had in mind. Let's start by considering what the Übermensch is not. Nietzsche contrasts the Übermensch with what he calls the "last man." The last man in a world in which God is dead and there are no objective values becomes lazy and apathetic (if there are no objective values, why care about anything?). He lives without passion and desire. He is a coward who lives solely for the sake of living. If there is no God, then who cares about life? In modern terms, the Last Man is a couch potato. In the Übermensch we find the opposite traits.

---

[1] Friedrich Nietzsche, *The Gay Science*, translated by Walter Kaufmann, in *The Basic Writings of Nietzsche* (New York: Random House, 2008).

The first mark of the Übermensch then is that he (or she, although Nietzsche probably wouldn't have considered that the Übermensch could be female) is passionate about life and is full of life. We certainly see this in Nucky Thompson. Nucky is no couch potato. He lives in a suite at the Ritz Carlton; he dines nightly at Babette's Supper Club, where it's the finest food, liquor, song and dance, and hobnobbing with the socialites, politicians, and elite of the crime world until the early morning hours; he spends some portion of each day enjoying the boardwalk, the seaside, and the people of Atlantic City; and he is passionate about women (whether he is married to someone else at the time or not).

So this is a good start for Nucky in his quest to be named Übermensch by us fans of *Boardwalk Empire* and Nietzsche. But it's just a start. Being Übermensch is a matter of meeting *all* the conditions laid out by Nietzsche, not just one or even some. A number of the characters in *Boardwalk Empire* meet the first condition.

Consider, for example, the Season Three protagonist: Gyp Rosetti. Rosetti is probably more passionate and full of life than any character in the series. In fact, he's so passionate that nothing counts as being a "little deal" for him. The smallest joke could lead to you getting a tire iron imbedded in your skull, as a well meaning good Samaritan learned in the opening minutes of Season Three. Rosetti is perpetually laughing; everything's a joke to him (except, of course, when he's flying off the handle in a fit of rage, and even then he tends to cackle a bit). He certainly doesn't lack passion.

We see the same type of passion (although to a considerably lesser degree) in Al Capone, Arnold Rothstein, and the delightfully nuts Mickey Doyle. We also see a great passion for life, albeit of a less libertine or gregarious sort, in Agent Nelson Van Alden. Perhaps, there's more than one candidate for Übermensch in *Boardwalk Empire*.

In addition to being passionate about life and full of life, the Übermensch must be strong and active. For Nietzsche, this means that the Übermensch must play an active role in forming the world in which he or she lives. The Übermensch shapes his or her life. While this certainly applies to Nucky—the Atlantic City he has inherited from the Commodore (his one-time mentor) bears only superficial resemblance to the Atlantic City he runs, and much of Nucky's Atlantic City has his stamp on it—the same can also be said for Rosetti, Rothstein, Capone, and Doyle. These mobsters sense the slightest bit of opportunity and they seize it outright. The Volstead Act is like a blank canvas for the ruthless to re-shape the world in the same way that the victorious kings of medieval Europe redrew boundaries on maps.

Here's where we must drop Agent Van Alden from the list of potential Übermensches. Van Alden is neither strong nor active (though he postures as both). Prior to leaving the Bureau of Internal Revenue, Van Alden exhibits precisely the Christian illness Nietzsche is rejoicing the death of. He is dogmatic and unwavering. More to the point he is a hypocrite, in that he preaches a hard Christian ethic, but violates the prime directive of that ethic—thou shalt not kill—by drowning a co-worker (Agent Sebso) who was "on the take." After leaving the Bureau, Van Alden is extremely passive with respect to the world in which he lives. He does whatever is necessary to survive and little more. He's lost all principle and conviction. He is the epitome of weak and ineffectual.

This brings us to the third mark of the Übermensch. For Nietzsche, once God is dead there are no objective values. To be more precise, according to Nietzsche there were never any objective values, and once God is dead everyone can recognize that there are no objective values. The fact that there are no objective values, for Nietzsche, is a good thing. It's not something to bemoan; rather it's something to be celebrated. Why? Because it's an opportunity to create your own values.

There are several examples of Nucky being a value creator in *Boardwalk Empire*. In the very first episode we see Nucky telling a whopper of a lie to the Women's Temperance League. After the speech Nucky tells Jimmy Darmody "Never let the truth get in the way of a good story." In Season Two we find Nucky attempting to console the congregation of an African American church on the heels of a KKK attack on Chalky White's bootlegging operation. Moments later Nucky is at an all-white church defending the actions of the Klan. In each case, Nucky is doing what is politically expedient for him to do at the time. This is not to suggest that any instance of lying or being "pragmatic" is an instance of creating one's own values, as some people are just liars (often such people will feel remorse or feel like they've done wrong, even though they might habitually lie, etc.), but in Nucky's case being politically expedient is what he values above all.

Another bit of evidence that Nucky creates his own values comes out in a discussion that he is having with Margaret about belief in God. Nucky asserts that he doesn't believe in divine retribution. More importantly, he does believe in "helping yourself with whatever is at your disposal." Here we see Nucky (in a qualified way) rejecting slave morality and Christian ethics.

The best evidence, however, of Nucky being a creator of values comes when he kills Jimmy—his one time protégé and someone he considered to be like a son. Jimmy knew that he was going to be killed and had no intention of fighting it (sort of an act of suicide by ticked-off mobster). Still Jimmy didn't want to let Nucky off entirely. He tells Nucky that killing gets easier at least until the booze runs out (one insinuation here is that Nucky has never actually done the killing before, when he's decided that someone should die). Nucky shoots Jimmy in the head, exclaiming "You don't know me James; you never did. I. Am. Not. Seeking. Forgiveness." Jimmy reasonably assumed that Nucky would feel insufferable remorse for killing someone he previously considered to be "like a son." Nucky's point is that however reasonable Jimmy's assumption was, it doesn't apply to persons who aren't guilt-ridden subscribers of Christian values.

What about our remaining candidates? While none of them appear to be operating strictly within the confines of a Christian ethic, it's not clear that any of them are creating their own values. Gyp Rosetti, for example, doesn't appear to have a value system at all. He merely reacts to whatever is directly in front of his face. If someone attempts to take something from him, as Nucky does when he chooses to limit his personal exposure by only selling alcohol to Rothstein, Rosetti reacts by hitting Nucky hard (by killing Nucky's drivers as they attempt to travel between Atlantic City and New York City). At one point, Rosetti beats up a priest (a duly appointed representative of God in Rosetti's mind) when he thinks that God is being unfair to him.

We don't have enough information on Rothstein, Capone, Doyle, or Lucky Luciano to state with certainty that they are not Nietzschean creators of their own values, but we don't have any evidence that they are. It does appear that along with other more minor mobsters seen in *Boardwalk Empire* they are operating according to the traditional mobster code of honor: omertà. There's a sort-of social contract at work here where all participants agree to

1. never co-operate with federal or local police authorities,

2. respect a code of silence, and

3. never interfere with the activities of others who have embraced the omertà.

While the omertà does not line-up with traditional Christian values, it constitutes an objective moral system nonetheless. Nucky, by contrast, does not always operate in accordance with the omertà; choosing to interfere with the activities of others whenever it suits him. Nucky is more puppet master, than good soldier.

The penultimate mark of the Übermensch is that he or she must be acting from a "dark side." As R.J. Hollingdale points out, Nietzsche teaches that "for virtue to be possible, the 'evil' passions must be allowed to flourish, for they are the only driving power."[2] This gets cashed out in a number of ways for Nietzsche.

First, the Übermensch must actually have a dark side. We've already seen that this is true of Nucky in spades.

---

[2] R.J. Hollingdale, *Nietzsche: The Man and His Philosophy* (Cambridge University Press, 1985).

Second, the Übermensch's love of life doesn't extend to individual lives. Or at minimum doesn't extend to every individual life. The Übermensch must be willing to sacrifice lesser lives for his own values. Almost immediately we see Nucky ordering the death of Margaret Schroeder's husband, Hans Schroeder, because he views Hans as having a lesser life (Nucky is pretty much spot on with this one: Hans Schroeder was a drunk who frequently beat his pregnant wife, and did so in front of their other children).

There are numerous other instances of Nucky sacrificing what he takes to be lesser lives throughout the series. There are hits on other mobsters, there are hits on politicians, but perhaps most egregiously, Nucky facilitated the rape of Gillian Darmody (Jimmy's mother) when she was just a child.

What about the (Super)Women?

To this point in the discussion we've dismissed all candidates for Übermensch except Nucky Thompson, but what about the women of *Boardwalk Empire*? Sadly the way the women characters of *Boardwalk Empire* are developed none come close. In fact each of the major female characters is primarily portrayed as a victim of sorts. Moreover, where Nietzsche has the Übermensch acting from a will to power (to use Schopenhauer's expression) that results in creation of values and a passion for life, the women of *Boardwalk Empire* are merely trying to survive. They are closer to the last man than they are to the Übermensch.

Margaret Schroeder, for instance, is a victim of Hans Schroeder's abuse. To escape she turns to Nucky, but finds herself subjected to a different sort of abuse—more psychological than physical. To cope, she actually has to compromise her own values.

Lucy Danziger, Nucky's one time lover, and Agent Van Alden's Baby Momma (as the kids are wont to say nowadays), is perhaps the weakest character on the show. She's literally imprisoned by Agent Van Alden and her only reaction is to become depressed and whine a lot.

Gillian Darmody probably comes closest to being the Übermensch, in that she is strong (despite being raped and impregnated as a child), is active (she wants a child so she claims her grandson as her own child), she doesn't seem to be acting in accordance with any particular code of ethics, and has a dark side which sacrifices "lesser lives" (just ask the poor fellow she injects with a lethal dose of heroin during a sexual encounter, purely in order to get his dog tags). But she fails to meet the "is passionate about life and is full of life" criteria. Gillian from start to finish just seems miserable. Also, although Nietzsche doesn't address this, it seems that being incestuous with one's own children ought to be a deal breaker. As there is no textual evidence for this in Nietzsche's works, instead of an argument, I'll just assert: just sayin'.

Well? Is He or Isn't He?

Thus far it appears that Nucky Thompson is a good candidate for being the Übermensch. But there's one more criterion that must be satisfied. The Übermensch must also be a teacher of the eternal recurrence. This raises two questions: what is the eternal recurrence and why must the Übermensch be a teacher of it. Let's begin with the second question, since it's a little easier to handle.

Since the Übermensch creates his own values, it's not possible for any of his actions to be unjustified—everything is morally okay. If that's true, then not teaching the eternal recurrence must be morally okay, too. And yet still Nietzsche is somewhat insistent on this point. Nietzsche's reason for being insistent is not a moral one, but, rather, an aesthetic one. The life of the Übermensch is aesthetically superior to both the last man and the Christian practitioner of slave morality. This requires the teaching of eternal recurrence, as doing so is an aesthetically superior way to live. It is the ultimate creative act.

So what is the eternal recurrence? In contrast to the Christian notion that people could somehow escape their present lives by attaining eternal life, Nietzsche wanted people to focus on their present lives. Nietzsche writes:

What, if some day or night a demon were to steal after you into your loneliest loneliness and say to you: "This life as you now live it and have lived it, you will have to live once more and innumerable times more; and there will be nothing new in it, but every pain and every joy and every thought and sigh and everything unutterably small or great in your life will have to return to you, all in the same succession and sequence—even this spider and this moonlight between the trees, and even this moment and I myself. The eternal hourglass of existence is turned upside down again and again, and you with it, speck of dust!"

Would you not throw yourself down and gnash your teeth and curse the demon who spoke thus? ... Or how well disposed would you have to become to yourself and to life *to crave nothing more fervently* than this ultimate eternal confirmation and seal? (*The Gay Science*)

So this demon provides a test for determining whether you appropriately value the life you have and whether you're living for that life (as opposed to living for some afterlife). You pass the test if you think living this life over and over for eternity would be the greatest imaginable blessing. This means that you have to live your life in such a way that you're satisfied with yourself and happy with your life.

Is Nucky Thompson a teacher of eternal recurrence? Is Nucky dedicated to helping people focus on the value of their present lives? In short, no. So Nucky, too, falls short of being Nietzsche's Übermensch. But fortunately, Nucky's story is not over. At this point, Nucky's story isn't over.

So there's still hope. It's true that Nucky will not likely ever become the teacher of the eternal recurrence, but if we've learned anything from Nucky it's this: never let the truth get in the way of a good story.[3]

---

[3] Thanks to Rachel Robison-Greene for suggestions, pointers, and comments on this chapter. Much of my discussion of Nietzsche's Übermensch was informed by the anonymous authors of *Friedrich Nietzsche in Plain and Simple English* (Golgotha Press, 2011).

3
Watching *Boardwalk Empire* with Freud

RON HIRSCHBEIN

Our fellow citizens have not sunk as low as we feared because they have never risen as high as we believed.

—SIGMUND FREUD, "Thoughts on War and Death"

We barely acknowledge Freud's presence: the show is more engrossing. He's no distraction—at first. "Put out that damn cigar!" is all we ask. After all, what can this voice from the dim past contribute to our viewing pleasure; can he tell us anything that we don't already know? Give us a break: we don't shock easily. We're comfortable twenty-first-century sophisticates. We already think psychologically—we psychobabble incessantly. Sure, we rationalize, but unlike Freud's subjects, we know what we're doing. In this cynical time we're masters of irony. Who doesn't realize there are always two reasons for things: very good reasons, and the real reasons?

Freud shocked his contemporaries by reducing everything to sex—or so we think. Are we scandalized? Well, "duh"; we like sex. We'd be stunned if a popular show *didn't* feature nothing-left-to-the-imagination sexual encounters—*Boardwalk* fills the bill. It's sexier than Freud, the proper Victorian gentleman, could ever imagine. And, if we catch Jimmy in reruns, a definition of Freudian slips comes to mind: "You say one thing but you mean your mother."

Seems we all speak Freud, now, correctly or not. We don't speak correctly. We speak a comic-book Freud, a pidgin psychoanalysis, a sanitized psychobabble that misses deeper, more disturbing insights. This Freudian primer offers a fresh take on the show. More significantly, it hazards unnerving insights about us and our limitless capacity for self-deception. Do the show's characters fascinate because they are markedly different from us—akin to alien beings from South Neptune? Or could it be that the likes of Nucky and Jimmy are avatars enacting that secret self that lives within? Read on. You'll find that, even now, the Father of Psychoanalysis doesn't comfort the afflicted; he afflicts the comfortable.

A Nation of Hypocrites

Freud begins by analyzing us; why are we watching *Boardwalk* in the first place? He calls us hypocrites—feeling a little discomfort? True, we may readily admit to a guilty pleasure: Those of us who abhor violence (or so we think) enjoy *Boardwalk*. But Freud won't let us off with such glib confessions. He gets in our face by indicting our profound, indigenous hypocrisy.

He might liken us to Agent Van Alden. (Don't he and his wife remind you of that *American Gothic* painting: that iconic image of the grim farmer with his pitchfork and humorless daughter?) But surely we're nothing like the FBI agent, introduced as the very embodiment of what Freud dubbed the anal-retentive personality: full of . . . self-righteousness, uptight, solemn, and doing his duty—so to speak.

Did you take Van Alden at face value, or did you suspect another self living in Van Alden, a true self aching for expression? Freud seldom takes anything at face value, let alone, Agent Van Alden. He knew that Van Alden's hypocritical pretense—the sober Christian gentleman—was unsustainable. Van Alden succumbed to *the* supreme pleasure, the explosive expression of that true self: "The feeling of happiness derived from the wild instinctual impulse untamed . . . is incomparably more intense than that derived from sating an impulse that has been tamed."[1] Don't you wish you could do so more often—maybe once?

Agent Van Alden partakes of the tepid enjoyment of dinner with his proper wife, but exalts in macho reverie as the restaurant is raided upon his command. Great sex with the not-so-proper floozy beats any respectful dalliance with his wife. Long repressed hatred toward colleagues emerges as he drowns Agent Sebso. And he responds to workplace bullying by burning his tormentor with a hot iron. Finally, he disposes of his old self along with that inconvenient body in his apartment. And so Agent Van Alden overcomes his hypocrisy; he becomes true to himself.

Unlike Van Alden, we only dream of expressing that other self living within. Could it be that, as Freud suggests: "We know that whenever we sleep we cast off our hard-won morality like a garment, only to put it on the next morning."[2] Tell the truth. Amid those nocturnal reveries, do you merely tell that attractive person that you like her—let's have coffee? Dreams are wish fulfillment: suddenly, you're a black belt in Kama Sutra. Speaking of wish fulfillment, responding to that humiliating encounter with that professor or boss, do you tepidly express your displeasure, or is it *Texas Chainsaw Massacre*?

Now Agent Van Alden is an unattractive character. We're put off by his uptight hypocrisy, and while lustful and violent, his true self is venal and petty. Bland, he lacks the panache of the colorful *Boardwalk* gangsters. Nucky and Jimmy are our avatars. Unlike Van Alden, they don't, for the most part—in the world according to Freud—come off as hypocrites. They're usually true to themselves—shamelessly self-serving. Freud might even deem Nucky psychologically healthy: he derives satisfaction from his work and intimate relations. In Freudian terms, psychological health does not necessarily reflect the highest morality.

---

[1] Sigmund Freud, *Standard Edition*, Volume 21, p. 79.

[2] Freud, *Character and Culture* (Collier, 1963), p. 119.

Nevertheless, the gangsters are free of certain conventional hypocrisy. They don't pretend they're free of prejudice, let alone tolerant. Freud describes a trait reinforced by the evolutionary process: the narcissism of minor group difference. Not unlike our narrow loyalties, the *Boardwalk* gangsters believe their ethnic group is superior because they happened to be born into it. Despite—or because of?—their marked similarities, Irishmen, Italians, and Jews, deride on another. (Thinking like a businessman, Nucky tries unsuccessfully to reconcile these groups.) In any case, our everyday narcissism craves the grandiose expression of these powerful movers uninhibited by civilized constraints—narcissism on steroids.

We're hypocrites and the Boardwalk gangsters are not? How can Freud deny the brazen hypocrisy of the likes of Nucky? In addition to deceiving his wife, he is not above deceiving his mistresses, to say nothing of his associates. Indeed, deception is standard operating procedure in Nucky's seaside empire.

Betrayal flows through *Boardwalk Empire* like illegal booze. Nucky and the others—even seemingly angelic Margaret—give cunning, duplicity, and dissembling a bad name. But Freud insists that, unlike us, Nucky's authentic where it counts. In our first encounter, Nucky, unlike Van Alden, is true to himself. He piously expresses the ideals of the Temperance Society, but we know better: he's not acting out of character. On the contrary, Nucky's duplicity serves his primal emotional needs: he's doin' what comes naturally.

Doin' What Comes Naturally

But what are these needs; what is human nature? The question percolates throughout the show. Contrary to popular misconceptions, Freud doesn't reduce everything to sex. On the contrary, in his mature writing, he stresses our radically conflicted nature: a fateful contest between Eros (the life-affirming instinct) and Thanatos (a destructive, death-affirming instinct). He notes his indebtedness to Plato throughout his mature writing:

According to our hypothesis human instincts are of only two kinds: those which seek to preserve and unite—which we call erotic, exactly in the sense in which Plato uses the word "Eros" in his *Symposium* . . . and those which seek to destroy and kill and which we class together as the aggressive or destructive instinct.[3]

Freud reframes Plato's three-part account of personality. Plato claims the personality is composed of competing passions, noble ideals, and a rational component which, ideally, can reconcile the passions with noble ambitions. For Freud, the passions (inherited from our animal ancestors) are the id; the ideals are conscience (superego); and the ego is the rational self we think we are.

The fix is in. The contest's outcome is determined by demands of civilization as soon as we come into this world. Our civilization creates and reinforces a repressed, albeit violence-prone, personality. (Making love isn't fit for primetime—only killing.) Erotic, life-affirming impulses are repressed: duty and necessity trump pleasure—just ask Agent Van Alden before the fall.

How often do we get to do what we love to do? Thanatos is encouraged, even celebrated, albeit confined to proper channels such as violence aimed at foreign enemies—real and imagined, and "making a killing" in the business world. Spectator sports and spectacles such as *Boardwalk* provide vicarious gratification. Other expressions of violence are strictly forbidden and severely punished lest we return to the state of nature and do what comes naturally.

It's wishful thinking to believe we're immune from the violent impulses that drive Nucky and Jimmy. Certainly not in warfare when killing with the imprimatur of government is condoned, even celebrated. Carefully controlled experiments illustrate the violent propensities reinforced by a repressive civilization. Milgram and Zimbardos's oft-replicated experiments reveal how readily that thin veneer of civilization shatters as a primal self emerges.

---

[3] *Character and Culture*, p. 141.

Milgram showed that fifty to sixty percent of randomly selected subjects will administer what they believed were painful, if not lethal, electric shocks upon other human beings.[4] Zimbardo's Stanford students played prisoners and guards. The experiment ended abruptly when the guards unexpectedly became sadistic brutes.[5]

Like the rest of us, Freud appreciates the obvious advantages of civilization. Like Hobbes, he believed that if people did what came naturally, life would be short, nasty, and brutish. Even so, he's painfully aware of the discontents. He laments: "civilization is the fruit of renunciation of instinctual satisfaction." Civilization gives us everything except happiness. Mick Jagger says it best, we "can't get no satisfaction." Worse yet, childhood trauma exacerbates the loveless life and festering violence of civilized humanity. We don't picture Nucky in a Norman Rockwell painting when we learn of his tormented childhood. And surely, a neurotic, seductive mother along with the carnage of the Great War didn't bring out the best in Jimmy.

Would we deny what's obvious—at least to Freud? We identify with Nucky and Jimmy: they're avatars of our true selves—expressions of our repressed human nature. How would *we* act if we could do what comes naturally? Nucky's and Jimmy's exploits provide the answer. Haven't you wished that you could utterly destroy your enemies and gratify lusts without a second thought? Freud reminds us that what we charitably call civilization is about the triumph of Thanatos:

> Men are not [simply] gentle creatures who want to be loved. . . .
> Their neighbor [whom they are commanded to love] tempts them
> to satisfy their aggressiveness on him, to exploit his capacity for
> work without compensation, to use him sexually without his consent, to seize his possessions, to humiliate him, to cause him pain,
> to torture and kill him. *Homo homini lupus.*[6]

---

[4] Stanley Milgram, *Obedience to Authority* (Harper and Row, 1974).

[5] Philip Zimbardo, *The Lucifer Effect* (Random House, 2007).

[6] *Character and Culture*, pp. 68–69.

A Higher Morality

But hang on. Unlike Nucky and his crew, don't we inhabit a different, an ennobling, moral universe? We subscribe to the civilized morality of the Ten Commandments. We're not barbarians. Freud indicts such claims as self-congratulatory civilized hypocrisy. Isn't it obvious:

> What no human soul desires there is no need to prohibit! It is automatically excluded. The emphasis . . . *Thou shalt not kill* makes it certain that we spring from an endless ancestry of murderers, with whom the lust for killing was in the blood.[7]

Not surprisingly, Biblical morality is gerrymandered to suit our proclivities. Given our propensity for violence, Jesus's pacifist injunctions in The Sermon on the Mount are ignored: who prays for their enemies? The apocalyptic fire and brimstone of the *Book of Revelation* befit our enemies. Freud quotes the poet Heine:

> Mine is a most peaceable disposition. A humble cottage . . . good food . . . flowers before my window, and a few fine trees before my door; and if God wants to make my happiness complete, He will grant me the joy of seeing six or seven of my enemies hanging from those trees. Before their death I shall, moved in my heart, forgive them all the wrong they did me in their lifetime. One must, it is true, forgive ones enemies—but not before they have been hanged. (Quoted by Freud in *Civilization and Its Discontents*, p. 49)

Did Nietzsche get it right? There was only one Christian, and He died on a cross.

While our demons triumph all too often, the contest between Eros and Thanatos is never fully resolved. Much to *Boardwalk's* credit—and to Freud's—characters are not portrayed as cartoon villains, evil to the core. That the conflict between Eros and Thanatos is ongoing, never fully resolved,

---

[7] *Character and Culture*, p. 129.

leads to a realization seen time and again in *Boardwalk*: "A human being is seldom altogether good or bad; he is usually "good" in one relation and "bad" in another, or "good" in certain external circumstances and in others decidedly "bad."[8]

We need believable avatars. How much evil can they stand? At times, Nucky and the others are conflicted and succumb to hypocrisy to deny their demons. To invoke a familiar Freudian notion, they put their actions in a favorable light by *rationalizing*. Like other gangsters, on occasion Nucky seeks absolution from his all-too-human impulses. He explains that killing is necessary, even heroic; he's a soldier, after all. Sometimes, he's just a businessman—nothing personal about killing, just business. Indeed, on several occasions, Nucky paraphrases Michael Corleone: Never ask me about the family business! Could it be that Nucky and the others are in denial?

Rationalizing that killing is nothing personal strikes Freud as a vestige of Victorian morality, squeamishness about passion. Nucky takes no conscious satisfaction in killing Jimmy; there are no bragging rights or rites. (We'll return to this episode—unconscious rivalry between fathers and sons—shortly; stay tuned.) Rival gangster Rosetti is less hypocritical and more authentic. Freud avers that trivial insults spark incendiary passion for revenge and murder. Time and again, we witness the truth of Freud's observation as Rosetti kills over trivial insults, real and imagined. No need to seek absolution for bludgeoning that gas station attendant or dousing that sheriff with gasoline and setting him on fire.

We readily identify with the characters because we understand, even sympathize, with them due to their pasts. Paraphrasing Freud, the child is the father of the man. Both characters are emotionally scared by abusive biological fathers. Worse yet, Jimmy was injured in mind and body by World War I. The war made Freud realize that humans are not simply "gentle creatures who want to be loved." Freud observed the war; Jimmy fought. They were never the same.

---

[8] *Civilization and Its Discontents*, p, 114.

"No event has ever destroyed so much that is precious in the common possessions of humanity, confused so many of the clearest intelligence, or so thoroughly debased what is highest."[9] Freud introduced Thanatos, the death instinct; no wonder he concluded that the lust for killing is in our blood.

Even so, strictly personal relations often show concern and affection. Nucky (a cross between Tony Soprano and Babbitt) cares about Margaret and her kids. And, at times, Nucky is relatively free of prejudice as his dealings with Chalky suggest. Interpreting his surprisingly generous response to the Commodore's African-American servant is difficult. (The servant poisoned her obnoxious, tyrannical boss.) Nucky gave the servant money and permitted her to escape. Did he do the right thing for the wrong reasons? Did he have mixed motives: compassion for the servant and hatred of his father?

Likewise, Jimmy (Holden Caulfield with PTSD) shows affection for kids, and befriends Richard, a disfigured fellow veteran. However, *Boardwalk* fans don't gather round the water cooler to commend Jimmy for being a nice guy: there's something about his relationship with dear ol' mom. No Freudian take on *Boardwalk* could omit mention of something near and dear to the Father of Psychoanalysis: the Oedipus Complex. Writing in *Rolling Stone*, McCall Polay recounts the obvious: "The entire episode was Freud's Oedipus complex writ large: Jimmy slept with his mother and killed his father."[10] Is the Complex fact or fiction?

Turning a Blind Eye toward the Oedipus Complex

As one of my students averred: "Not even my father is sexually attracted to my mother!" Whether the male child is cap-

---

[9] *Standard Edition*, Volume 14, p. 275.

[10] McCall Polay, "Boardwalk Empire Re-Cap, Oedipus Wrecks," *Rolling Stone* online: www.rollingstone.com/movies/news/boardwalk-empire-recap-oedipus-wrecks-20111205#ixzz2HMCrIMiC.

tivated by Freud's most infamous notion, the Oedipus Complex, is controversial. According to Freud, the healthy individual overcomes the Complex, and even those who don't, rarely act upon it.

The legendary Oedipus was blind; he didn't know what he was doing. I suspect the show's writers and producers could see what they were doing: Could it be they attempted to boost ratings by portraying Jimmy's embarrassing relations with his mother? As Polay recounts the episode:

> From the moment the two enter the room, you can feel what's coming. Jimmy starts off the scene half-naked thanks to a bloody shirt. Toss in a vulnerable Gillian ("I'm the loneliest person on Earth"), and you have a recipe for one of the most sickening moments in television history.

Or does the episode offer a back-story to account for Jimmy joining the army? Both of the above?

Polay describes the incident as the Oedipus Complex writ large: an understandable conclusion for those unfamiliar with Freud's unnerving account of the Complex writ large in collective psychology. Freud narrates what he believes is the oldest psychology, *the* primal, perennial driving force of history; the very script of *Boardwalk*—the revolt of the sons against the father. In his neglected *Group Psychology* he speculates:

> The primitive form of human society was that of a horde ruled over despotically by a powerful male. I attempted to show that the fortunes of this horde have left indestructible traces upon the history of human descent . . . connected with the killing of the chief by violence and the transformation of the paternal horde into a community of brothers.[11]

Parricide enables the band of brothers to seize patriarchal property, especially women. Margaret is introduced as a

---

[11] *Group Psychology and the Analysis of the Ego* (Norton, 1959).

strong, liberated woman only to become Nucky's property. Gillian, as Rosetti learns, is no one's property. Are we warned that strong, independent women are practitioners of evil? (Freud is rightly derided for his attitude toward women.)

Boardwalk recounts this ancient narrative. As Freud reminds us, the masterpieces of Western literature all deal with the same subject—parricide. In addition to the *Oedipus* saga, he has *Hamlet* and *The Brothers Karamazov* in mind. Indebted, perhaps, to these classics, *Boardwalk* improvises the murderous cunning of the "Oldest Psychology," the core of our being—the drama of the primal horde. Not only does Jimmy slay his biological father, he and his brothers in crime revolt against his father-figure. It's a sin they can live—and die—with. If the series continues, would we be surprised to watch Nucky's children conspiring to slay him? And so it goes.

Are we, as Freud insists, bedeviled by repressed impulses of violence and lust; do we fantasize about ridding ourselves of those bosses and politicians? In the process, we may become bosses, politicians, and the like. In so doing will we give credence to Freud's jeremiad: "In reality, there is no such thing as eradicating evil."[12]

Is *Boardwalk* cathartic? Could it be that Nucky and Jimmy provide vicarious gratification enabling *us* to live with sin?

---

[12] *Character and Culture*, p. 113.

4
How to Be Happy on the Boardwalk

PATRICIA BRACE AND MARIA KINGSBURY

The raucous, glittering, touristy, corrupt Atlantic City of *Boardwalk Empire* doesn't seem a likely place to happen upon profound philosophical endeavors. The characters there, at first glance, seem far more concerned with food and fashion and fads—the stuff of consumerism and base desire. However, the characters in *Boardwalk Empire* grapple with a question that towering philosophers have returned to for eons: what is happiness, and how can a person become and remain happy?

Aristotle, that great progenitor of the Western philosophical tradition, notably puzzles over this question in his *Nicomachean Ethics*.

> Is happiness acquired by learning, or habituation, or by some other form of cultivation? Or is it the result of some divine fate, or even of fortune? (*Nicomachean Ethics*, lines 1099b9–10)

Despite their separation by thousands of years, the flawed and seemingly shallow characters of *Boardwalk Empire* probe their universe with the same strategies of trying to learn or earn happiness, of trying to acquaint themselves with people who will make them happy, or by trying to change the circumstances of their fate so that happiness is within reach for them.

Aristotle, were he a subscriber to twenty-first-century HBO, would be shaking his head in consternation, however: these characters will never achieve happiness. They are fated to fail, not only because they get caught up in appearing happy, but because they don't know what happiness is.

A Great Mind Confronts a Great Question

Happiness, according to Aristotle, is a complex condition and different for everyone, but it is foremost a "stable dynamic," a self-sustaining, habitual action that yields its own rewards and perpetuates itself. The actions leading to happiness are of a specific sort: "It is the activities expressing virtue that control happiness," says Aristotle (*Nicomachean Ethics*, lines 1000b10–11). Unfortunately, while desiring the stability of the happiness that arises from virtue, the characters of *Boardwalk Empire* instead pursue its superficially similar, but ultimately very different associate, pleasure:

> The many would seem to conceive the good and happiness as pleasure, and hence they also like the life of gratification. Here they appear completely slavish, since the life they decide on is a life for grazing animals. (lines 1095b19–20)

Pleasure, while it has many of the same external characteristics as happiness, is wildly unstable, prone to bouts of excess, and dependent upon purely consumable goods.

Common sense and Aristotle readily acknowledge that certain material goods and privileges are necessary for happiness:

> Happiness evidently also needs external goods, as we said, since we cannot, or cannot easily, do fine actions if we lack the resources. For, first of all, in many actions we use friends, wealth, and political power just as we use instruments [objects or tools]. Further, deprivation of certain external conditions and goods— e.g. good birth, good children, beauty—mars our blessedness; for we do not altogether have the character of happiness if we look utterly repulsive or are ill-born, solitary, or childless. (lines 1099a31–33, 1099b1–4)

The material "instruments" of happiness are insufficient to produce happiness on their own. Dazzled by the shining, perfumed, ego-boosting pleasures of power, money, and influential relationships, it is easy to lose sight of virtue in the quest to maintain and acquire more "instruments." As a result, a life becomes wildly unstable, subject to the mercurial whims of backroom politics, petty grudges, and changing fashions. While they might appear to be in control of their own fates, these characters are most certainly not.

Happiness on the Boardwalk

Atlantic City itself, according to historical accounts and its portrayal on *Boardwalk Empire*, is the perfect place to perpetuate a culture of ostentatious material and behavioral excess. Instead of the balances Aristotle argues are most desirable, the culture in Atlantic City is oversized, thrill-seeking, and visually glamorous.

Atlantic City overflows with the novelty of varied virtuous purposes, from the premature infants displayed in their miraculous incubators in the front window (so showcased to glean money to save undersized babies' lives), to the glittering, domineering signage promoting Gillette's razors, an oversized consumer ploy, to Babette's glitzy, stylized nightclub that harbors the schemes and trysts of Atlantic City politicians. The characters who stroll the boardwalk, however, when followed into their hotel rooms and row houses and kitchens, are left with only the things they think will make them happy—not the stable dynamic Aristotle describes.

All of the characters in *Boardwalk Empire* are caught up in the obsessive quest for pleasure, but three: Nucky Thompson, Chalky White, and Margaret Schroeder, provide especially layered and vivid examples. They commodify—make materialistic and expendable—intangibles Aristotle exempts from the economic sphere: love and friendship, learning and sophistication, and spiritual goodness. What ought to be virtuous activities aimed toward stable happiness become, because they cannot conceive of any other way, instruments used to achieve pleasure. The material pursuits embraced by Nucky, Chalky, and Margaret eventually come to dominate them and obliterate all but shallow appearances of the virtuous action Aristotle argues is necessary for happiness.

Dressing the Part: Nucky Thompson and Chalky White

At first glance, Nucky Thompson and Chalky White fit Aristotle's mold of happy men: they publicly demonstrate virtues of temperance, generosity, friendship, and continence, and they *seem* to have the best interests of their communities—and, in their crossing of racial lines—even the United States—in mind. However, their friendship, as viewers quickly discover, is based entirely upon their mutual desire to remain in power and in possession of material wealth.

Nucky cares about Chalky no further than his ability to control the African American population, and Chalky values Nucky's ability to provide him privileged social access and prestige, as "A Return to Normalcy" demonstrates when Nucky pays off Chalky to secure the African American vote.

Appropriately, appearances are crucial for both men: Nucky and Chalky are fastidious—and expensive—dressers, wearing bold colors and patterns that stand out even on the boardwalk, just as they stand out from other flashy politicians in their ostentatious generosity and responsibility to their constituencies. However, viewers discover that Chalky and Nucky are uneasy occupants of their tailored suits and costly shoes. Just as buttons fall off, shoes wear out, and fabric gets stained, so do Nucky and Chalky's attempts to find happiness in things and appearances lead only to decay and emptiness.

Finding a Beautiful Love Magnet

Behind Nucky's charming demeanor and cutthroat political philosophy—those things that make him the boss of Atlantic City—is his belief that friendships must be cultivated to achieve happiness. Aristotle would not disagree with this, but Nucky accumulates people and connections with a single-minded determination that exceeds the ideal, virtuous mean that Aristotle strongly espouses. Instead, Nucky conceives of these relationships as goods to be bought and sold, obliterating the virtuous, happiness-inducing friendships that would heal Nucky's childhood scars of abuse and pain.

Nucky "buys" with money and titles the people he ought to care for regardless of their potential utility. His mentee and surrogate son, Jimmy, and his brother, Eli spring immediately to mind, but perhaps the most striking instance of his materialistic approach to relationships is in his dealings with Margaret, the woman he eventually marries and entrusts with his wealth and fame.

Nucky's brother, Sheriff Eli Thompson, encapsulates Nucky's attitude in "Paris Green," screaming in frustration, "This is my life on the line! I got eight kids. You waltz around town like it's a circus, gettin' your ass kissed. Nobody cares about you; they only care about what you can give 'em. And that includes your Irish chippie who you've just handed a blank check." Eli isn't far off; throughout *Boardwalk Empire*'s first two seasons, Nucky showers Margaret with material wealth. He appears to truly care about her and her children, and perhaps even wants to, but he can come no further than maintaining the appearance of a happy, stable home life, marrying Margaret only when it is politically expedient, giving Teddy money instead of disciplining him, and exploiting Margaret's adeptness with words for his own political means ("Hold Me in Paradise").

While joking with Margaret about the "wonderful love magnet," a physical item that draws affection from others, described in *The Road to Oz*, a book by L. Frank Baum that Margaret is reading to her children, Nucky observes that such an object would make winning an election cheaper. When he asks Margaret if she plans on voting for Warren Harding—his candidate—for president, she references Nan, Harding's delusional mistress. Nucky responds that if only good men were elected there would be no leaders. Margaret puzzles over what qualities ought a leader to have, if not goodness. Nucky cites utility to his supporters. All relationships, all obligations to one another as human beings to Nucky's mind, are founded on pragmatic use. Relationships are just instruments for passing pleasures.

Chalky White and Keeping Up Appearances

Chalky, while he mirrors Nucky in many ways, is more keenly aware of the superficiality of his façade of happiness. Chalky, no matter how he dresses or whom he associates with, cannot escape his black skin, though his family embodies all of the material qualities of the socially rising white middle class: his son is going to college and plays classical piano, his wife, Lenore, is light-skinned and stylishly dressed, and his daughter is dating a boy who stresses his unfamiliarity with the "country ways" Chalky knows still itch beneath his skin. Chalky, like Nucky, only gives the appearance of stability and power; in reality, he is harboring deep-seated misconceptions about what will bring him happiness.

A scene that memorably illustrates the ways Chalky creates the appearance of a virtue and uses it to exert pleasurable power is in "Ourselves Alone." Chalky has been jailed on Nucky's orders "for his own protection," literally imprisoned by his desire to maintain his connection with Nucky. At first, because of the prestige of his connection with the Thompsons, Chalky is housed apart from the rest of the African American prisoners, and he sits in his impeccable suit and with a thick book in his hands, recognizable to literate viewers as Charles Dickens' *David Copperfield*. As he appears to read, he is goaded by another African American prisoner, a nicely dressed—but not as nicely as Chalky—man who introduces himself as Purnsley. The two men have an exchange brimming with veiled insults clothed in folksy drawls. Purnsley asks Chalky about their most visible difference, the book in Chalky's hands. Chalky tells him that it's *Tom Sawyer*. Purnsley apparently "knows his letters," and steps up his insults of Chalky, feigning incredulousness when another man chimes in that his conversant is "Chalky White." All the while, Chalky calmly turns pages, seemingly worlds above Purnsley's words.

When a white man needs a cell, though, Chalky is put in with the rest of the black men. The next time viewers see him, he appears to have made progress in his book, but when Purnsley mockingly asks him to read aloud, Chalky simply refuses. Eager to expose the reality underlying Chalky's educated and superior appearance and exert his own power, Purnsley grabs the book, leaving a page ripped off in Chalky's hand, and calls him "just another jigaboo in a jail cell." Immediately, but languidly, Chalky addresses by name the other men in the cell, one by one. They beat up Purnsley, and pick up the mutilated book from next to his bloodied face. Chalky does not choose to exercise his power when Purnsley insults his person or makes insinuations about his wife, but only when Purnsley rips into a material thing that Chalky considers intrinsic to his façade.

Choosing How Much Sin with Which to Live

While Chalky and Nucky can be observed constantly working to maintain the level of material pleasure they have already achieved, Margaret Schroeder evolves, and it is through her story, with its dramatic rises and falls, that the truly unstable nature of the pursuit of pleasure rather than genuine Aristotelian happiness is revealed. Margaret wants nothing more than stability, and yet it's denied her at every turn.

The dress shop is a transformative place for Margaret, and one through which she comes to acquire and perform all of those things that ought to make her happy. Here she is first introduced to the appearance of happiness that things— beautiful clothes, lingerie (the perfect balance of things taken off and put on), the close proximity to important peo- ple— can bring, and the subsequent power that wielding them yields. She goes from gratefully taking a job that Nucky procures for the welfare of herself and her children and accepting insults from the French shopkeeper to having Madame Jeunet, the shopkeeper; beg her for help in keeping her store.

In between, viewers see Margaret steal, blackmail, feign magnanimity, and finally use her own body as an object to exercise power over Nucky. None of this brings her stability, though—instead, she finds herself with even less than she had prior to setting foot in that dress shop. Margaret's acquisition of things ultimately does nothing to bring her honest, self-perpetuating happiness. As Esther Randolph, the woman prosecuting Nucky for his crimes asks Margaret, in "To the Lost," "What has he ever given you besides money?" Margaret uses that money to try to buy off unhappiness, most poignantly when her daughter Emily is diagnosed with polio. In "Georgia Peaches" she takes all of Nucky's gifts and money she has secreted away and delivers them to her parish priest, hoping that action will convince God to spare her daughter.

Here we must pause and wonder why, instead of being happy with what they've already acquired, characters over and over again opt to consume huge amounts of alcohol, have risky sex, dress in ostentatiously expensive clothes, and parade about their relationships with powerful people. Aristotle has an answer: Virtue is an activity of the soul. He says, "The virtues arise in us neither by nature nor against nature. Rather, we are by nature able to acquire them, and reach our complete perfection through habit" (lines 1103a24–25). So, virtues are seemingly accessible to these characters with their energetic pursuit of happiness. However, Aristotle emphasizes, "A state of character arises from [the repetition of] similar activities. Hence we must display the right activities, since differences in these imply corresponding differences in the states. It is not unimportant, then, to acquire one sort of habit or another, right from our youth; rather, *it is very important, indeed all-important*" (lines 1103b21–25, emphasis added).

From the outset, neither Nucky, nor Chalky, nor Margaret has had the opportunity to learn and practice the virtuous behavior that they need to find true happiness. All have come from broken places: abuse in Nucky's case, racial terror in Chalky's, and abandonment and spousal abuse in Margaret's. "We all have to decide how much sin we can live with," Nucky tells Margaret in "A Return to Normalcy." This is where the characters are left, not choosing between one virtuous action and another, or virtue and vice, but rather the amount of sin—that burden upon the soul—that they will endure. The combination of derelict upbringing and decadent lifestyle choices leads them, as Aristotle would predict, to places nowhere near happiness.

Two important characters from *Boardwalk Empire*, Jimmy Darmody and Richard Harrow, are both World War I veterans who bring a different perspective back with them from their time in the trenches. Their ethical and unethical approaches to life's big questions differ from Nucky's, Margaret's, and Chalky White's.

Richard Harrow and the Happiness of the Tin Man

For you cannot quite regard a man as happy if he be very ugly to look at, or of humble origin, or alone in the world and childless, or—what is probably worse—with children or friends who have not a single good quality or whose virtues died with them.

—ARISTOTLE, *Nicomachean Ethics*, lines 1099b1–5

"How does it feel? To have everything?" Richard Harrow asks Jimmy Darmody in the Season Two opening episode of *Boardwalk Empire,* "21". Like Jimmy, Harrow is a World War I vet, and while Jimmy's PTSD manifests itself through his internal conflicts (along with a *serious* sort of double Oedipal complex, more on that later) Harrow's literally shows on his face. Horribly wounded in the war, half of his face is reduced to skin stretched over skull, empty eye socket, half a mouth, nose, and damaged voice box. He covers this with a metal mask fashioned to look like the remaining half of his face, including moustache and glasses. He feels like half a man as well, incomplete and cut off from the American dream. It's clear to anyone who can see that Harrow only pretends to be whole and happy. Unlike Nucky or Chalky or Margaret, Harrow's attempts to conceal his brokenness, to acquire the material objects needed to be whole and stable, fail in front of everyone.

Harrow is a sniper, an elite marksman who can kill from a distance, but is equally effective at close range with any weapon handy (we see him kill with several types of guns, and even use a knife to scalp a man). As an assassin and guard he has value to Darmody, Nucky, and the Commodore. After Jimmy procures him his heart's desire by asking the prostitute Odette to help him lose his virginity at the Chicago brothel, Harrow pays him back by assassinating the man who disfigured Jimmy's prostitute girlfriend, Pearl, which had resulted in her suicide.

Pearl and Richard are both visibly without one of the instruments of happiness—decent looks—in an age when appearance is everything. We see evidence that Richard Harrow also had dreams of his version of the good life through the collages he makes by taking clippings and cutouts from catalogues, *Good Housekeeping* magazines, and newspapers showing an idealized life with family and material possessions.

In this way, Harrow is acquiring objects that represent happiness and wholeness, but these are further removed from happiness's realization than the things gathered by Chalky (for one). Harrow's acquisitions aren't tangible things or relationships, but two-dimensional *representations* of those things Aristotle mentions as objects necessary for happiness. He places these representations over book pages, likely the ones his sister continues to send him that he has no interest in reading. As he tells Jimmy when they first meet ("Home"), "It occurred to me, the basis of fiction is that people have some sort of connection; and they don't." However with his collages he is literally rewriting the text of his life—creating a new fiction on top of another fiction. As Margaret does not, Harrow recognizes that the material goods themselves surrounding happy people are empty, but he also understands that appearance is everything in 1920s Atlantic City. Harrow believes himself to be cut off from the reality of happiness because he cannot sustain even its illusion.

Know Thyself

Friendship is a vital component in Aristotle's description of happiness. Through companionship with like-minded and equally virtuous people, Aristotle claims, happiness can be achieved. Like all virtues, the habit of being a good friend (and, by extension, good family member), must be cultivated from a very young age. Once more, by exploring the contrast between Jimmy and Richard, we find that the mere appearance of having a stable, rich family life does not translate into its reality.

Jimmy came into the world through the rape of his thirteen-year-old mother by the influential Commodore, and from then on his relationships continued to get increasingly complicated. Nucky was his father figure when Jimmy was growing up, taking him fishing and spending time with him, acting out his "Uncle Nucky" persona. Jimmy was ignored by the Commodore for most of his life, until he became useful as a pawn in the power game between Nucky and the old man. Jimmy's most important relationships are of a pragmatic, power-based nature from his earliest days, and this fosters in him a desire for power and wealth, to be someone important and respected. His upbringing, as Aristotle predicts, thus corrupts him and causes him to betray (among many others) the man who has been his closest friend his whole life, Nucky. Season Two portrays the two men locked in a competition for control of Atlantic City, with threats coming from external sources, such as federal prosecutors, fellow mobsters, and even their respective family members.

Jimmy's friendship with Richard Harrow is markedly different. Perhaps because of their shared war experiences and wounds—and, likely, Richard's own upbringing in a stable home—the two form a bond that Aristotle would admire (though he likely wouldn't consider the numerous assassinations and smuggling they carry out particularly estimable). By appearances, they're an unlikely pair, far from the beautiful ideal that Jimmy cultivates in other aspects of his life with his ostensibly perfect family and home, his stylish clothes, and his extravagant gifts. Harrow is visibly broken, but the unshakable devotion he has for Jimmy, his desire for nothing more than meaningful human connection, elicits in Jimmy true Aristotelian virtue: without any consideration of himself, he tries (sometimes clumsily) to respect and take care of Harrow, procuring him female companionship, offering him a place in his own family, and finally pleading with him to "be happy."

The Tin Woodman

In "Emerald City," Harrow uneasily inserts himself, an awkward, artificial appendage, like his mask, into another ostensibly "happy" family, Nucky's and Margaret's. After an attempt on Nucky's life, Richard is assigned to be a body guard and stays in their home. He sleeps, without his mask, on their downstairs couch, dreaming of a walk on a beach with Odette as a whole and therefore happy man. Then Odette starts screaming. Harrow wakes and finds the screamer is actually Margaret's young daughter, Emily, who has wandered downstairs and is frightened by his maskless visage. Even a child recognizes that Richard doesn't "belong" in a stable, happy household.

One evening Margaret is reading another one of the Oz books, *Dorothy and the Wizard in Oz* to Teddy and Emily. Harrow appears in the doorway, and after some hesitation, Margaret invites him to listen as well. When she shows them all an illustration of the Tin Woodman (though she misspeaks and says "Woodsman"), Richard taps his mask to show them he is the Tin Man and he needs some oil. In doing so, he aligns himself with the fictional figure that sought not material possessions from the Wizard, but a heart with which to feel emotion again. This is the perfect metaphor for the hollow man Richard Harrow, who also lacks the organic means to achieve Aristotelian happiness. It allows the children to put a recognizable label on him, the brave Tin Woodman who helps Dorothy find her way home, but it has much greater depth of meaning in the context of the series.

References to external artificiality or triviality belying true human virtuousness (and through that virtuous action eventual happiness) surround Harrow; his likeness to the empty Tin Man and the disfigured Tin Soldier from children's stories is referenced several times in the series. When they first meet (in his first appearance, "Home"), Jimmy Darmody is reading a book titled *The Tin Soldier*, written in 1918 by Temple Bailey. The title is an allusion to the Hans Christian Anderson fable about a molded toy tin soldier who falls in love with a ballerina doll, in part because like him she has a disability; both have only one leg. Through a series of misadventures they both end up swept up into the fire and while he melts into the shape of a heart, symbolizing his undying love, she merely burns to cinders and ash, implying she never really loved him or was faithless.

Harrow's life and character have been subsumed by the literal and figurative artificial mask he is required to wear; what seems to have replaced Richard's emotions and relationships is his skill at killing. Death is his art as much as the collages he creates. His most valued possessions when Jimmy first meets him are his guns and his masks. Harrow pulls a souvenir of his tour of duty, a German sniper's mask, out of his satchel telling Jimmy if he doesn't have it with him he becomes anxious. The solid metal mask is painted black with only two tiny holes for the eyes.

At his lowest point, Harrow realizes he can't ever have what he wants; that the one girl he's ever slept with did it because, as Al Capone reminds him when Richard asks about her, "she's a whore." He decides that no decent girl will ever find him desirable, that he can never have the things which are necessary for happiness, the things that fill his collages.

Harrow recognizes that proximity to the Aristotelian "instruments of happiness" isn't enough to actually reach a stable, happy state. He knows that, despite appearances, Jimmy and Angela aren't truly happy: Angela, Jimmy's wife, was not faithful to him when he was gone in the war or in Chicago—she took a female lover, and later takes another. Jimmy was unfaithful to her, both with his own mother in the incestuous encounter that provoked his enlistment and later in Chicago with the young prostitute Pearl. His power in Season Two comes not from his own initiative, but from his father, a twisted relationship since he is the result of the Commodore's rape of his thirteen-year-old mother. He has to betray his surrogate father, Nucky, to gain this power, so he is going against honor owed to a parent, and then later also murders his father (who was trying to stop him from choking his mother to death—even though she kind of deserved it) the ultimate betrayal: patricide.

Into the Woods

When the sadness of Harrow's life becomes too much for him, he makes the same choice as Pearl, to end his life with a gun, choosing his sniper rifle, in the second season episode, "Gimcrack and Bunkum." At first we don't realize that suicide is what Harrow is planning. Driving out to the woods, he takes a walk, has a picnic, and then removes his mask to feel the wind on his face and look up at the trees and clouds. When he puts the barrel of the rifle in his mouth we are shocked. Then a rather mangy looking mostly German Shepherd dog steals his mask, sending Harrow on a frustrating chase.

He could have easily just shot the dog, or just let it go—he really won't need the mask when he's dead, after all. Instead he dashes after it through the woods, yelling "I need that!" and then loses track of the dog and falls, exhausted and weeping, to the forest floor. He's found by one of two men (hunters?) in the woods to whom the dog seems attached, although they refuse to claim ownership, demonstrating straight away their distance from Atlantic City's glittering materiality. One of the men clearly understands what Harrow had been going to do and tells him that the woods are for living, not death. The other offers him a ride home in his car.

Going "into the woods" is often used as a metaphor in literature for entering into darkness and tribulation, from Tolkien's Mirkwood and Dorothy's journey to Oz to Steven Sondheim's musical meditation on what happens after happily ever after, with their common theme that no one can find their way out of the woods alone. With help, Harrow is able to make it back out of the woods, and it is this realization that human connections for the right purposes (Aristotle would call them virtuous purposes) that allows Harrow to begin his journey back to happiness, to let him set aside the material impediment of his mask.

In a telling scene directly after his aborted suicide attempt, Harrow and Jimmy meet up and it's clear that both are troubled. When asked by his friend if there is a problem, Harrow asks, "Would you fight for me?" Jimmy doesn't hesitate—he comes closer to Richard, looks him in the eye and says, definitively, "Of course I would; right down to the last bullet." Harrow's response, "Then let's go to work," and Jimmy's gentle hand to Richard's head reminds Harrow of a truth that Aristotle articulates: "Friendship is a virtue, and besides is most necessary in our life" (lines viii1 1155a2–3).

Meeting Jimmy and accepting his gestures of friendship changes Harrow's life. The human connections he earlier disparaged as non-existent are now at the center of his life. His first act of loyalty to Jimmy is to avenge Pearl's suicide by killing her slasher. He bonds not just with Jimmy, but with Jimmy's wife Angela and his young son, Tommy. Angela treats him with respect and affection, at one point asking him to sit for her to sketch and he is comfortable enough with her that he allows her to draw him without his mask ("What does the Bee Do?").

When Angela's killed, it is eventually Harrow who will avenge her by killing her slayer, Manny Horvitz, in Season Three, with a shotgun blast directly through his eye, mimicking Harrow's own war wounds ("Resolution"). In Seasons

One and Two, he also takes care of the mess after Jimmy murders his father, the Commodore, helps Jimmy scalp a man who insulted him, goes with him to round up the killer Klan members and deliver them to Chalky White, kills two of the D'Alessio brothers, and assassinates crooked politician Jim Neary. Richard is a good (but very scary) man to have on your side when the bad stuff happens.

Terminator as Guardian Angel

After Jimmy's death in the second season finale "To the Lost," Season Three finds Harrow still in Atlantic City because of his affection for Tommy, the last remaining member of the family he cared about so deeply. Harrow chooses the virtuousness and truth of real friendship over superficial respectability, and takes a job working for Jimmy's mother Gillian at her new brothel as a bartender/bouncer. In "Ging Gang Goolie" he joins a veterans' group and through it meets a nice woman, Julia Sagorsky, who he later takes to an American Legion dance (his first ever) where she shocks him by kissing him out on the dance floor, evidencing the weakening of his mask as a barrier between him and true happiness (The Milkmaid's Lot").

In "Sunday Best," accompanied by Tommy, Richard also goes to her home for Easter and when Tommy runs afoul of Julia's father Paul by innocently playing with the toy tin soldiers he finds in Julia's dead brother's room, it is Harrow who, very fatherly, defends the boy. Walking on the boardwalk afterwards, they are mistaken by a photographer for a family, and have their picture taken. Richard turns in profile, showing his face, not his mask for the photo. For a brief moment, Harrow has the image of his heart's desire and is able to embody, to experience, the kind of contentment and happiness represented in his collages. It is contentment, a stability, for which he will forego all other morality and materiality to protect, as the Season Three finale, "Margate Sands," in which Harrow takes on an entire house full of gangsters to rescue Tommy, makes clear.

This Is the Only Way We Could've Ended

The predictable results of what the American Founding Fathers deliberately but confusingly call "the pursuit of happiness" are revealed through the lives and choices made by the characters of *Boardwalk Empire*. Nucky and Chalky are left with only beautiful suits to show for their actions, not stability and self-worth. Margaret's complete faith in the power of things makes her blind to the decay of the virtues that might actually bring her happiness. Jimmy's quest for peace ends in his violent death at the hand of his surrogate father, Nucky. Harrow abandons all sense of respect for human life—even his own—in his attempt to solidify the human relationships that he desires more than anything else.

Treating the Aristotelian instruments of happiness as objects to be acquired and appropriately used leads only to loneliness and failure. The audience is then left wondering, like Aristotle, what the flawed characters of *Boardwalk Empire* think they know: what *is* happiness, really?

Part II

Medicinal Liqueurs

5
Does It Matter that *Boardwalk Empire* Is Historically Inaccurate?

Rod Carveth

An important type of TV programming is historical fiction. There are generally two types of historical programming, the docudrama and the "based on" movie or series. The idea of a docudrama is to incorporate historical fact with narrative techniques in order to create a more-or-less accurate depiction of an actual event that will appeal to a wide audience.

The docudrama has been a staple of film and television since the 1980s. A hybrid of the documentary and the dramatic film, docudramas present viewers an interpretation of reality that contains some degree of historical accuracy and factual authenticity.

One category of docudrama is the "headline" docudrama. "Headline" docudramas are based on events that have occurred much closer to their airing, usually within five years. These docudramas usually follow one of two basic plots. The first plot revolves around tales of adversity, where the principals display courage and persistence and achieve some form of triumph, such as *The Ryan White Story*, which portrays the boy's struggle with AIDS.

The second basic plot centers on tales of crime, often involving greed or lust or both. An example of this type is *Beyond Control: The Amy Fisher Story*, a true story of the Long Island teenager who tried to murder the wife of her lover. One of the primary selling points of these docudramas is that they are "based on fact" or "based on real-life events."

The second type of docudrama is the historical docudrama, a fictionalized retelling of a period of history, such as *Patton: The Final Days*. While many docudramas have achieved critical acclaim, they have also prompted ethical debates about how facts can be stretched in order to create more drama. This has been seen in the film *Nixon*, as well as docudramas such as *The Path to 9/11*, *The Reagans*, and *The Kennedys*. For example, *The Path to 9/11* was marketed both domestically and globally as the "official true story" of the events that lead to the September 2001 World Trade Center attacks. At first, the docudrama's producers argued that the movie's script was largely based on the US government's *9/11 Commission Report*, but later backed away from that claim.

While they are not documentaries, docudramas have an ethical obligation to depict the facts that are important to the historical event. In order to facilitate telling a good story, a certain amount of creative license is often taken. The problem is that this creative license can lead to a distortion of the history that is being portrayed.

The "based on" movie or series version of history takes far more liberties with the facts, to the point of often not letting the facts get in the way of a good story. For example, *The Holocaust* miniseries tells the story of the Holocaust from the perspectives of the (fictional) Weiss family of German Jews and that of a (fictional) rising member of the SS, who gradually becomes a merciless war criminal. The miniseries blended fictional characters with real-life ones (such as Heinrich Himmler and Adolf Eichmann). Though the series scored numerous awards, critics such as Elie Wiesel decried the series as "semi-fiction" and distorted history.

Boardwalk Empire: Real or Reel?

Boardwalk Empire similarly distorts history. About four minutes into the initial episode of *Boardwalk Empire*, Atlantic County's treasurer, Nucky Thompson, is speaking to the Women's Temperance League. Nucky regales the ladies with a tale about a boy's efforts to survive the winter of 1888, after the boy's alcoholic father deserted the family. The boy, Nucky says, killed a group of wharf rats with a broom handle for food.

Upon hearing this, the crowd gasps. Then Nucky reveals that he is the little boy, and the crowd bursts into applause. As Nucky leaves the event, his assistant Jimmy Darmody questions Nucky about the veracity of the story.

"First rule of politics, kiddo," Nucky responds. "Never let the truth get in the way of a good story."

In many ways, this describes *Boardwalk Empire*. The show focuses on the Prohibition-fueled rise of organized crime in New Jersey during the 1920s. Created by Terence Winters (of *The Sopranos* fame), the series features highly visible executive producers (such as Martin Scorcese—who directed the first episode—and actor Mark Wahlberg) and a big budget (the pilot episode reportedly cost a reported eighteen million dollars). The series is based on the book, *Boardwalk Empire*, written by historian Nelson Johnson. The series' main character of "Nucky" Thompson is based on the real-life exploits of Enoch L. "Nucky" Johnson, who ruled Atlantic City through politics and crime for thirty years.

Similar to Nucky's story, *Boardwalk Empire* engages in a delicate balancing act with fact and fiction. Like a person having an affair with two equally appealing lovers, the series is unable to stay monogamous to either fact or fiction. On the one hand, *Boardwalk Empire* is a show about a real time period and a real place, and the series strives to be historically accurate with settings, dress, language, etc.

On the other hand, the series mixes truth-based and fiction-based plotlines, though it is often unclear where the real history ends and the "reel" history beings. Most of the central series characters are "based on" real life people, albeit with fictionalized names. The main character Nucky Thompson is based on Nucky Johnson. Nucky Thompson's mentor is Louis "The Commodore" Kaestner, who is based on real life

Atlantic City politician Louis "The Commodore" Kuehnle. Nucky Thompson's brother, Sheriff Eli Thompson, is based on Nucky Johnson's brother Alfred Johnson. Finally, Nucky Thompson's assistant, Eddie Kessler is based on Nucky Johnson's assistant, Louis Kessel.

The "based on" characters interact with real historical figures. Many of them are gangsters. Al Capone, Johnny Torrio, and Big Jim Colosimo appear, as do New York counterparts Arnold Rothstein and Charles "Lucky" Luciano. Other historical figures are U.S. Attorney General Harry Daugherty and Treasury Secretary Andrew Mellon.

Therein, for the series, lies an ethical dilemma. Because it is difficult to know where truth ends and fiction begins (and vice versa), it is possible that viewers of *Boardwalk Empire* may actually take the series as being fact, when it's not.

Some historical inaccuracies are careless mistakes, such as when Arnold Rothstein picks up a coffee cup and there's a bar code on the bottom of the cup, or when federal agent Van Alden receives a divorce decree from a federal court A more glaring error concerns the Ritz-Carlton hotel, where Nucky Thompson does most of his business. The Ritz-Carlton did not exist when Prohibition began, and the hotel seen in the show looks nothing like the real Ritz-Carlton. The hotel opened in June 1921, a year and a half after *Boardwalk Empire* is supposed to begin.

What I am taking issue with is the "history" in *Boardwalk Empire*. For example, in the very first episode, real life character Al Capone is given a military service background when he never was in the military. Gangster Charles Luciano is referred to as "Lucky" in the series first episode, set in 1920. Luciano earned the "Lucky" nickname by surviving a 1929 stabbing. During the series' second season, when Nucky visits Ireland to trade machine guns for Irish whiskey, the discussion of the negotiations between the Irish and the British completely misrepresents the roles of Eamon de Valera and Michael Collins.

There are ethical concerns about changing "real" history into "reel" history, particularly since those viewers not familiar with 1920s Atlantic City (probably a vast majority of the series' viewers) could believe that what happened in the series actually happened in real life. Part of the problem is that *Boardwalk Empire* is not just loosely based on the life of Nucky Johnson. What confuses the issue is that real historical characters play central roles in the series. The roles of two *Boardwalk Empire* characters exemplify this problem, Al Capone and John McGarrigle.

Will the Real Al Capone Stand Up?

Al Capone is introduced in the first episode. Nucky's protégé, Jimmy Darmody, strolls up to a short guy leaning against a dark car in the nighttime. They strike up a conversation about their time in the war. "What's your name?" Darmody asks. "Al," the short guy replies. "Al Capone."

Capone figures prominently in the first three seasons of the series. English actor Stephen Graham portrays Capone. In real life, Capone was a large man, 5' 10" and of sizeable girth. Graham is much shorter (5' 5") than the real-life Capone. More importantly, when he is introduced into the series, he is comparatively laid back—unlike the mercurial real-life Capone.

Beyond the lack of physical resemblance of the real-life Capone to Graham's portrayal is the historical accuracy of Capone's relationship to Nucky. While it's clear that Capone visited Atlantic City, Capone biographer Jonathan Eig suggests it is highly unlikely that Capone had much of a relationship with Nucky. For example, in the series premiere of *Boardwalk Empire*, Capone is seen to be a major part of the shoot-out in the Hammonton woods near Atlantic City. At that point in time, the real-life Capone was nowhere near Atlantic City. It is also completely untrue that Capone helped come to Nucky's rescue (as shown in Season Three) in order to battle gangster Gyp Rosetti.

There are other historical inaccuracies as well. In the sixth episode of Season One, Capone is shown living in an apartment in Chicago with his wife and son and mother. According to Eig, Capone's mother was not yet living in Chicago at that time, and Capone's wife was not as submissive as she's portrayed in the series. Capone's son, Sonny, is portrayed as being entirely deaf at the age of two years. In real life Sonny contracted an infection (likely from Capone's syphilis) that left him only partially deaf from the age of seven.

Capone's mentor, Johnny Torrio, is represented in *Boardwalk Empire* as an aging gang leader who's ready to let Capone take control. Torrio was more sophisticated than the character in the show, and more careful about his image. Torrio arranges the assassination of Jim Colosimo in order to take over Chicago, yet he's torn between wanting to make peace with the other gangs and realizing that there's enough money for everybody. In real life, Capone was a bookkeeper whom Torrio plucked from New York City to work for him in Chicago. Under his tutelage, Capone quickly rose to become Torrio's partner and eventually took over the business after a failed assassination attempt scared Torrio back to a life in Italy. Torrio was more of a pacifist than Capone, and was always trying to teach Capone to be a diplomat. But the series doesn't portray Torrio as much of a mentor.

The series did get one important thing right about Capone. *Boardwalk Empire*, is about Prohibition-era Atlantic City, and the real-life Capone, like many other characters in *Boardwalk Empire*, owes his rise to Prohibition, and the profits that resulted from bootlegging. Capone, then, is portrayed as a symbol of the former driver who becomes a nationally known gangster making it big selling illegal liquor. When Prohibition began in 1920, Capone was just one of Johnny Torrio's many employees. But by 1925, Torrio would retire and leave Capone in charge of a vast criminal empire built on Prohibition money.

The Muck of the Irish

While Al Capone was a real person, John McGarrigle (played by Ted Rooney) is not. McGarrigle is a fictitious Irish politician. He works as a fund-raiser for Sinn Fein and is a leader in the Irish Republican Army (IRA).

McGarrigle is introduced in the Season Two episode, titled "Ourselves Alone." Sinn Fein, the name of the political wing of the IRA, is Irish for "Ourselves Alone." McGarrigle visits Atlantic City as part of a fundraising trip around America to help support Sinn Fein and thereby the Irish Republican Army. He dines with Nucky and Margaret during his trip. McGarrigle receives a donation from Thompson, and arranges for his bodyguard, Owen Sleator, to remain with Nucky, when he returns to Ireland.

In the episode "Battle of the Century," Nucky travels to Ireland, looking to make a deal with the IRA leadership by trading surplus army weapons for Irish whiskey. There Nucky learns that McGarrigle's youngest son was killed shortly before while fighting for the IRA. As a result, McGarrigle is not interested in trading whiskey for arms, though many of his IRA comrades are. McGarrigle's refusal to deal with Nucky leads to his being killed by his own men. After this assassination, the IRA begins to trade liquor for weapons with Nucky.

During the episode, McGarrigle observes that Sinn Fein president Eamon de Valera is traveling to London to negotiate terms for peace with the British government. Nucky asks McGarrigle what is on the negotiating table and McGarrigle explains that the British are offering a free state. Later in the episode it is noted that de Valera goes on to sign a truce with the British leading to the Anglo-Irish treaty that causes a split within the IRA and the Irish Civil War.

The history here is highly misleading. For one thing, de Valera himself left Ireland for eighteen months from June 1919 to December 1920 to raise over five million dollars in the United States. In June 1921 the British Prime Minister wrote to de Valera to invite him to London to discuss a truce. De Valera accepted this invitation and went to London, and after days of negotiations signed a truce on July 9th 1921 ending the war and leaving the door open for further negotiations about the future of Ireland. When those negotiations eventually began in October, de Valera did not return to London and sent negotiators, including Michael Collins, in his place. This second set of negotiations led to the signing of the Anglo-Irish treaty in December 1921, which was then ratified in Ireland in January 1922.

I Knew Nucky Johnson and You're No Nucky Johnson

Another big problem with the "reel" history of *Boardwalk Empire* is in comparing Enoch "Nucky" Johnson, Atlantic City's real-life politics and racketeering boss, to HBO's fictionalized "Nucky Thompson." The real Nucky, who ruled Atlantic City from 1911 to 1941, was a tall, muscular, imposing, man who swam five or six days a week to keep in shape. Nucky Johnson weighed about 225 pounds and stood more than six feet tall. He had a voice to match his stature and used his physical presence to meet and mingle. On the other hand, actor Steve Buscemi, who plays Nucky Thompson, is not physically imposing. The actor has a high-pitched voice, stands just five feet, eight inches tall, weighs under 150 pounds and is very slight.

There are some similarities. A widower whose love of his life died early on in their marriage, Nucky Johnson liked socializing and living large, eating and drinking in Atlantic City's nightclubs and restaurants, freely spending, employing maids and drivers and tipping big as a matter of habit.

Nucky Thompson also loses his wife early on in his marriage (she died of tuberculosis), and as the series opens, carries on with an active social life (though he is far less gregarious than the real life Nucky Johnson). He subsequently has an affair with, then marries (for legal convenience), Margaret Shroeder, a widow whose husband Nucky had killed.

In addition, Nucky's mentor is Commodore Louis Kaestner. In the same way that Nucky is Jimmy's mentor, Nucky learned from the Commodore, who is basically retired after a stint in prison. The real-life Nucky was mentored by a businessman, Louis Kuehnle, known as "The Commodore" due to his chairmanship of a yacht club. Kuehnle had been friends with Nucky's father, the county sheriff. When Kuehnle went to prison in 1913 for awarding his own firm contracts as chairman of the Water Commission, Nucky Johnson took over as the Republican Party power broker for the region. He helped establish the system of kickbacks from illegal industry to local government.

What Makes Good History May Not Make Good Television

The biggest issue, however, is that physical violence is an aspect of almost every installment of the series. Frequently, the violence is carried out by either Nucky or one of his closest followers.

That's not really how it worked in Atlantic City, according to Nelson Johnson, author of the original book *Boardwalk Empire*. "They are doing their best to do historically accurate fiction," Johnson has observed, explaining that by "accurate fiction" he meant creating a storyline that captures the essence and possibilities of the Prohibition era in Atlantic City, not necessarily the verifiable details.

The real violence was the threat of economic ruin if Nucky's organization withheld the job security so many Atlantic City residents needed. Instead of physical violence, the people who crossed Nucky and his organization lost their government jobs, they were ostracized, their businesses not patronized, their operating licenses were pulled, or they were raided and shutdown by complicit police who were a part of the organization. The organization's pervasive clout meant that physical violence was seldom needed. As Nelson Johnson observed,

> Atlantic City's corruption was organic. Most employment in Atlantic City was seasonal, so many people had to scrounge for survival for the rest of the year. Having a full-time year-round job was a big deal that bought loyalty. It was organized crime, but without the violence.

Nucky Johnson held power in two distinct circles—organized crime and politics—and was able to make those two spheres one thing. Under Prohibition, Atlantic City was one of the few cities where people could in practice openly drink alcohol, and drink they did. Atlantic City became one of the most popular holiday destinations and won the nickname the "World's Playground." Johnson took a percentage of every gallon of alcohol sold.

In real life, Nucky Johnson was also famously helpful to the poor (including African Americans), and they helped him right back by providing the votes he needed to steer senators and congressmen into power. It was Nucky Johnson's organization—the Republican Party—that promoted the racketeering that financed his and its political power. One of the most important facts about the real Nucky Johnson was the interlocking organization he built, starting on the street and precinct level, then to the ward level, not just in Atlantic City, but in nearby towns and throughout county government. To keep the organization working, Nucky made it a point to directly meet and interact with the rank-and-file members of the organization, to know about their loyalties and the details of their lives.

The political organization Nucky Johnson oversaw extended to the statehouse, the governor's office, the state Supreme Court and the operations of the local newspaper. Johnson benefitted from this political power for three decades until a couple of documents Johnson thought had been flushed down the toilet led to Johnson's arrest and conviction for tax fraud.

On the other hand, this version of organized crime is hard to translate to entertaining TV. Ironically, the first half of the first season does focus much more on corruption and its attendant economic violence, than organized crime. But, the important organizing work of Nucky Johnson is not portrayed through the character of Nucky Thompson. When the series begins to shift focus to the rise of organized crime brought about by Prohibition, the bodies begin to fall.

The Docudrama Effect and the Ethics of Reel History

Boardwalk Empire is overseen by executive producer Terence Winter, a writer and executive producer for *The Sopranos*. The story the show tells is a melding of fictional and real characters interacting amid mostly factual events.

"We try to be as historically accurate as possible," Winter said in Hollywood. "I can't give you an actual percentage, but I would say we're running in the high ninety [percent] in terms of historical accuracy. There were a couple of occasions where events did not take place on exactly the day or month that they took place, but in terms of, you know, storytelling, taking creative license, [the changes] don't alter history in such a huge way that I was reluctant to do it."

Nucky's name change, Winter said, was made partly to thwart Google. "Obviously, everybody knows what happened to Al Capone and Luciano and Rothstein, and I was afraid that, if people started to Google the real Nucky Johnson, they would [get] ahead of the story, and they would know what became of Nucky or when did he live and die [sic] or what he did or didn't do."

The major ethical concern, however, is how well the depiction of "reality" in the series fairly represents the actual events. Due to the narrative constraints of telling a good story, dialogue is often invented, characters are composites of several people, and even certain occurrences are made up. The act of adapting an event to standard narrative formulas changes reality in the process. It is this changing of reality that can cause viewers to misperceive how events actually happened.

In addition, while Terrence Winter may believe his series is about ninety-percent historically accurate, he is significantly overstating the case. The settings, the clothing, and the dialogue are historically accurate, but the depiction of the actions in Atlantic City are not. Winter is trying to have it both ways—to have the liberty to tell stories that will ensure continued viewership while at the same time claiming the drama is "realistic." Research shows that viewers don't always know the difference. Giving viewers a false re-telling of history is unethical.

Little research on the impact of televised historical fiction on the audience has been conducted. What has been conducted shows that viewers might confuse historical truth with historical "truthiness" (as Stephen Colbert notes). Researchers who tested the effects of the 1983 movie *The Right Stuff* (about the first US astronauts) found that subjects who knew little about Senator John Glenn became significantly more positive about him as a person and presidential candidate. Other researchers measured effects of exposure to the 1987 miniseries *Amerika*, that depicted life in the Midwest ten years after a Soviet takeover of the United States. They found that exposure to the program was correlated with a shift in attitudes toward less tolerance of communism and greater acceptance of increased US military strength. They also found that viewers' stereotypes of American citizens on average became more positive. Other social scientists found that effects of *All the President's Men* and *Washington: Behind Closed Doors* respectively were largely restricted to issues specifically addressed in these productions. When researchers examined the effects of *The Day After*, a drama about life after a nuclear war, they concluded that exposure to the program affected the importance of nuclear war in the subjects' minds and also influenced the amount they knew about nuclear war. Subjects' political attitudes about the U.S. government, however, did not change. Perhaps most importantly, studies suggest that viewers who are least familiar with an event or issue "learn" the most from these docudramas. The problem is that what viewers learn may be a misrepresentation of reality.

Given the research, it's important for TV producers to keep in mind that while they may know what's fact and what's fiction, the audience may not. The historical image presented of Atlantic City in the 1920s is one where considerable violence brought on by organized crime occurred. The reality of the history of Atlantic City is very different.

6
What's Wrong with Agent Van Alden's God?

ROBERTO SIRVENT AND NEIL BAKER

Agent Nelson Van Alden waits alone in a long, arched hallway, the feeble glow of electric lamps casting little puddles of orange on the pale hospital walls. A nurse approaches and he raises his head steadily, though turning it to face her seems to be more of a struggle for him. His hands, folded gingerly in his lap, begin stirring in an uncharacteristically nervous shuffle as she informs him that Agent Clarkson is ready to be seen in his room at the end of the hall. Clarkson had suffered serious burns in an explosion two episodes earlier, and the audience can't help but share Van Alden's horror as they get a glimpse of what's left of the agent's body.

Just as Van Alden gathers his wits enough to break his stare and lower his head, presumably in prayer, Supervisor Elliot and Agent Sawicki appear through the door and join him near Clarkson's bed. "Jesus Christ," Elliot exclaims, "How is he still alive?" Van Alden answers his supervisor's question: "He loves the Lord, sir." "It seems that's a pretty one-sided relationship," Elliot responds. Van Alden, his horror becoming anger, immediately reprimands his superior for his blasphemy. "Even the doctors, men of science, agree that his fate rests in God's hands, not theirs."

But isn't Supervisor Elliot's question a fair one? If we assume with Van Alden that there is a God who loves people like Agent Clarkson, and who is concerned about their fate, is it reasonable to think that he would choose to allow these things to happen, or even *cause* them to? Like many in his time and ours, Van Alden appears to believe that the course history takes is strictly determined by the will of God. Yet is it really possible to believe that God is good, while at the same time believing that God is the ultimate cause behind all the pain and hardship—all the evil—we see in the world?

Van Alden's God

Let's start by taking a closer look at the way Nelson Van Alden thinks about God, and about how God interacts with the world. We just considered a scene from "The Age of Reason" in which Van Alden intimates his belief that in the end, it is God who is responsible for determining the course of peoples' lives. We might call this way of thinking about God *strong providential theology*, and as we can already begin to see, it's distinguished by the belief that God's power to bring about his will in history is unlimited and absolute. Stated differently, strong providential theology strives to emphasize the doctrine of God's *omnipotence*.

This particular way of viewing God is, in fact, quite common today. We can recognize Van Alden's view in phrases like "God is in control" and "It's all part of God's plan." Sometimes we can even see it cropping up outside of religious contexts in the common expression, "Everything happens for a reason." Still, notwithstanding its popularity, does strong providential theology really represent the best way of understanding God's relationship to events in history?

Theology, like any other "ology," is not a static, solidified collection of ideas; instead, it's the product of a long history of conflicting viewpoints and heated debates. As such, strong providential theology can be understood as one stream of thought among many other competing streams, and it will be helpful if we trace this stream back to some of its most important historical sources. One of the distinguishing features of strong providential theology is *determinism*, the view that events are bound to happen, or "determined" to occur just as they do before they actually take place. Determinism figures prominently in the thought of the great Christian theologians Augustine (354–430) and Thomas Aquinas (1225–1274). It becomes more pronounced during the Reformation era, however, as a result of the work of the Protestant Reformer John Calvin (1509-1564).

Calvin describes for us his thoroughgoing and radically deterministic doctrine of divine omnipotence in his most important work, *The Institutes of the Christian Religion*. In no uncertain terms, he writes that human beings can "accomplish nothing except by God's secret command," and that they "cannot by deliberating accomplish anything except what he has already decreed within himself and determines by his secret direction."[1] Thus, when Van Alden says that Agent Clarkson's fate rests entirely in God's hands, Calvin would be in full agreement.

In addressing the subject of human mortality, Calvin pulls no punches: he boldly asserts that death "was not only foreseen by God's eye, but also *determined by his decree*"[2] (Chapter 16, emphasis added). In applying his assumption of divine omnipotence, Calvin is nothing if not consistent.

We've already seen how strong providential theology has made its way into our everyday speech about God, though it's not very often that we think through its implications as rigorously as Calvin did. Yet we're subtly asked to do this kind of reflection many times throughout the plot of *Boardwalk Empire*. A poignant example comes to us in the episode "Blue Bell Boy." Margaret encounters a married couple on the boardwalk that had suffered a dangerous miscarriage. With regard to his wife's trauma, the husband rather jauntily informs Margaret that "It was God's will, and when the time is right, we'll try again." Of course we recoil at his blithe indifference to his wife's pain, but before we do we should ask ourselves whether our way of understanding God is

---

[1] John Calvin, *The Institutes of the Christian Religion*, Book 1, Chapter 18.

[2] *Institutes*, Chapter 16. Emphasis added.

really all that different. For instance, if I were to thank God for the safe delivery of my healthy child, wouldn't I also have to conclude that it was God who was responsible for the miscarriage in the next room? Like Calvin, the husband on the boardwalk holds a theology that is deeply troubling, but consistent.

It is Agent Van Alden, however, who demonstrates for us what is probably one of the most disturbing aspects of this sort of theology. Turning our attention back to "The Age of Reason" we find Nelson returning home, but not to his wife. Van Alden had promised to take care of Lucy until her child—his child—is born, and in the meantime he has the prostitute hidden away in a cramped apartment. She's begun to develop a case of cabin fever, however, and now she finally asks Nelson for some time away. But Van Alden can't have that; he can't risk having Lucy be seen around town in her present state. Thus, Nelson chooses this moment to remind her that this pregnancy is a "charge from God," and that her desires are more or less irrelevant.

Even if Lucy is fooled by Van Alden's holy façade, the audience isn't. The theological smokescreen that Nelson has thrown up in this exchange is no uncommon tactic for those who hold to a form of providential theology, and for many religious groups it's become instinctive. Rather than accepting the consequences for his recklessness and infidelity, here we see Nelson shifting the responsibility for Lucy's inconvenient pregnancy over to God. What's more, he even uses this strategy to manipulate Lucy into complying with his restrictive demands. As this episode begins to make clear, when strong providential theology is involved, it's often difficult to distinguish between God's will and the will of the one who claims to know it.

Nowhere is this disconcerting element of Van Alden's theology clearer than in the eerie baptism scene of "Paris Green." Nelson has regarded Agent Sebso with no veiled suspicion ever since the agent shot a witness, allegedly out of self-defense, and Sebso is fed up with it. Yet when he reveals his intention to put in for a transfer to Detroit, Van Alden informs him that there's still one thing he can do in order to regain the trust of his superior. Agreeing to Nelson's terms, Agent Sebso follows him into the woods, where they find the congregation they had encountered by chance earlier in the episode. Sebso, a Jew, was to partake of the rite of baptism. Leading his subordinate into the water, Nelson leans to dip Agent Sebso below the water's surface—and he keeps him there, until Sebso's convulsions begin to fade as the life gradually leaves his body. Raising his eyes, the agent utters a confident and stoic prayer: "Thou has fulfilled the judgment of the wicked." In this moment Van Alden has no doubt that his hands have become God's instruments, and flashing a badge and a gun at the stupefied congregation, he leaves confident that in Sebso's horrific death the will of God had been realized.

Getting Around the Problem (Trying to, Anyway)

We've spent some time thinking about Van Alden's understanding of God and about some of the implications of viewing God as he does. Now we'll take a look at one important approach that's been used in attempt to hold onto the doctrine of omnipotence while avoiding some of the problems we've talked about. To do this let's return once more to the scene we began with in "The Age of Reason," where we found Van Alden at Agent Clarkson's bedside.

Recall that one of the difficulties we found with Van Alden's perspective was that it seemed to imply that God was the ultimate cause behind Clarkson's suffering. Now suppose for a moment that we were to suggest to Nelson that God, rather than *causing* Clarkson's pain, merely *allowed* Clarkson to experience the negative consequences of other peoples' decisions. The Dutch theologian Jacobus Arminius (1560–1609) proposed something similar in order to make Calvin's ideas a bit more palatable. Arminius contended that the "providence of God is subordinate to creation," or the normal order of things in the world. He draws from this the belief that God's private will "should not impinge against creation, which it would do, were it to inhibit or hinder the use of free will in man."[3] According to Arminius then, the suffering we see in the world is the unfortunate but inevitable result of our free ability to make our own moral decisions. God could intervene and save the day, but for the sake of preserving our freewill, he chooses not to.

Upon first glance, this seems like a pretty reasonable alternative. First of all, God no longer reminds us of a nasty kid with a magnifying glass, frying poor Agent Clarkson like an ant just because he can. Moreover, God still seems to retain a good deal of omnipotence. Even if he chooses not to determine history in order to keep our freewill intact, he nevertheless retains his prerogative to do so. But is God really off the hook here? We might compare this way of talking about God to a situation in which a child disobeys her parent by running into the street. Our hypothetical parent sees an oncoming car at some distance, yet he decides not to save his child on the grounds that doing so would violate the child's freedom to disobey. Most of us would find the parent's decision repugnant of course, and by analogy there still appears to be something morally troubling about Arminius' God. Thus it seems we have some work to do yet if we're going to get away from the problems of strong providential theology.

But wait a minute—aren't we forgetting something here? Might the troubles we've noted in Calvinism and Arminianism alike fade away if only we recall the old adage, "God works in mysterious ways"? The argument might go something like this. Yes, the parent we described above should save the child, since he has no reason to believe that by saving his child he might inadvertently bring about more harm than good. But of course, the case is different with God. Whereas we have only limited perspectives, God sees the "whole picture" of history. While to us his actions (or inac-

---

[3] *The Works of James Arminius,* Volume 2, p. 460.

tions) may seem mysterious, even malicious, ultimately God has the good of the world in view. We'll call this line of reasoning the 'mysterious ways' argument.

We're willing to recognize that as human beings, our perspectives on history are anything but complete. Still, we're not sure that the mysterious nature of God's will is quite enough to excuse his playing a part in excessive human suffering. Moreover, we don't think that such a picture of God looks much at all like the one that the Abrahamic religions have traditionally called their adherents to worship. While it's true that some theologians have argued that we should worship God simply because he's God, more often religious men and women have worshiped because they find within God's nature characteristics that are *worthy* of worship. Let's consider the exchange between Van Alden and Supervisor Elliot in "The Age of Reason" to see how the 'mysterious ways' argument makes God's worship-worthiness difficult to make out.

Here's where Elliot's apt response to Van Alden's idea of God becomes important in our discussion. Recall his complaint that if Clarkson really does "love the Lord," it appears to be a pretty one-sided relationship. He meant this as a sarcastic quip of course; but though he may not realize it himself, Elliot's statement illuminates for us a profoundly troubling aspect of Van Alden's God that we've yet to consider. On some reflection we can see that in fact, Clarkson's relationship with God is one-sided in a deep and philosophically significant way: Van Alden's God doesn't appear to share a common moral vocabulary with the beings he's created. Indeed, for Van Alden's God, the definition of a loving relationship apparently involves burning one's beloved to a crisp!

We can begin to understand then why a theology that overemphasizes the mysterious ways of God presents serious problems for the religious person's ability to worship. It may be that God has some grand scheme for history and humankind, a scheme we mortals are too limited to comprehend. Even so, it hardly seems reasonable to expect the victims of outrageous moral evil to find anything admirable or worship-able about a God whose idea of love and justice is the source of the evil they've experienced. We who live on this side of the Holocaust have been made acutely aware of this. Clearly then, something has to give, and we think that something may be the doctrine of divine omnipotence.

Nucky's God

We've now begun to see that the problems inherent in Van Alden's conception of God won't be easily done away with. But in order to salvage God's moral character, are we really willing to say that God isn't omnipotent after all? Those who favor a form of providential theology argue—rightly—that if God is limited, then there's no guarantee that he'll be able to rid the world of evil. Nevertheless, some have suggested that in order to continue believing in a truly benevolent God, we need to call the doctrine of omnipotence into question. Rabbi Harold Kushner writes, "I can worship a God who hates suffering but cannot eliminate it, more easily than I can worship a God who chooses to make children suffer and die, for whatever exalted reason."[4] If then we do decide to follow Rabbi Kushner's guidance on this point, what might we be able to say about God's relation to history?

It's here that the corrupt politician and gangster Nucky Thompson may just have something to teach us about the nature of God. In the episode "To the Lost" Margaret complains that Nucky's God "asks nothing" of him, and his response is intriguing. Though he seems unsure of the truth of many of the particular doctrines of his Roman Catholic faith, nevertheless his "God" does indeed ask a few things of him. He asks, for instance, that Nucky love his wife and his family, and that he care for and protect them. Now what we find interesting here is not what Nucky thinks about God in a metaphysical sense, that is, whether he believes God exists in this or that way, or not at all. Indeed, it's probably impos-

---

[4] Harold Kushner, *When Bad Things Happen to Good People* (Avon, 1981), p. 134.

sible to nail Nucky down on any abstract theological question we might ask him.

But from what we can tell of Nucky's views, God appears to be something like that drive we all feel to act rightly. Nucky's God is, roughly, the impetus he finds within himself toward whatever is morally good. The question of whether to follow this impetus, however, is left open for him, and we know that on many occasions he decides not to follow it. What we wish to highlight here is the fact that while Nucky's God does *ask* certain things from him, he doesn't seem to have the ability to *coerce* Nucky into doing them by force.

In the twentieth century a new branch of theology known as "process theism" began its work from this very proposition, that God's way of acting within history is characterized by persuasion rather than force. Process theologians agree with Rabbi Kushner insomuch as he believes that God simply doesn't have the power to violate the freedom of the individual to make his or her own moral decisions. Their position implies, of course, that it's not within God's power to ensure a happy ending for history. After all, process theology takes its name from the guiding conviction that instead of being "above" history, God is intimately involved in the unfolding of history.

Process theology has strengths which we can see when we look at the problems with Van Alden's thoughts about God. First, the holy façade Van Alden puts up in "The Age of Reason" wouldn't fool anyone in a church that taught process theology. By convincing Lucy that her pregnancy is a sacred "charge" from the Lord, Van Alden is able to free himself from any of responsibility he might otherwise have had in the situation. But if God acts within history by means of persuasion rather than coercion, then it's clear that Van Alden must share in at least some of the responsibility for the pregnancy. Even if it really is God's will that Lucy should become pregnant, Van Alden's will is instrumental in bringing it about.

But the most prominent benefit of process theology is that it does not portray God as a moral monster. Because they see forces at work within the world powerful enough to counter the will of God, process theists are able to say in an honest and coherent way that the evil we experience runs counter to God's desires. Far from being evil's source, the Process God works alongside his creation in order to eliminate evil from the world.

Ungodly Games

We want to conclude by admitting the difficulty of the subject that we've taken up. Just as thoughtful religious (and non-religious) men and women have disagreed with each other in the past, so we recognize that the future is not likely to bring with it any final resolution to this matter. Still, we think most *Boardwalk Empire* fans will agree that Van Alden succeeds in making providential theology a hard pill to swallow, and *something* about his view of God needs re-thinking.

In the episode "Sunday's Best," we find Gyp Rosetti in the middle of an impassioned monologue before a painting of the crucified Christ. It's Easter, but Gyp isn't celebrating. He thought he'd finally gotten ahead, only to have his business take a major hit at Nucky's hands. Now his family's all he has left to comfort him. We saw them all earlier in the episode sitting down to an Easter meal: his meddling mother-in-law, his nagging wife, his obnoxious daughters, all of them squished into a tiny tenement. No, Gyp is not cele-brating today.

We understand then why this Easter afternoon finds Gyp in a church, screaming and spitting. How emasculated he must feel. So he cries out, "Put it in front of me, then take it away. Why would you do that? Just to screw with me! What kind of sick fuck thinks that way? I'm supposed to trust you?" Then, when a priest makes the mistake of interrupting, Gyp punches him and turns to the collection bag, demanding whatever else there is.

Gyp shares Van Alden's belief in an omnipotent God of course, though he appears to understand something about this God that Van Alden either fails to see or refuses to admit. Many have found themselves in situations not unlike Gyp's, where suffering seems needless and meaningless, and the fleeting spark of hope seems actually to have been a cruel joke played at your expense.

At such times, it's hard not to wonder whether God might only be playing games with us for his own amusement. Just to screw with us. And it's at times like these that we'd just as soon be left out of the hands of Van Alden's God.

7
Blaming Nucky Thompson

MICHAEL DA SILVA

In "Return to Normalcy," the final episode of Season One, Jimmy Darmody forms an alliance with his father, the Commodore, and newly reinstated Sheriff Eli Thompson to replace Atlantic City treasurer Enoch "Nucky" Thompson as *de facto* city boss. Jimmy's betrayal, which provides the main plotline for Season Two and leads to Jimmy's downfall, is doubly shocking: Jimmy never got along with his father and grew up with Nucky in a parental role.

The possibility of betrayal, however, was hinted at in the previous episode, "Paris Green." After the then-ailing Commodore hints that Jimmy, not Nucky, should be running Atlantic City, Jimmy is reluctant to betray his mentor and friend. This changes when Jimmy's mother, Gillian Darmody, tells Jimmy about the circumstances of his conception. When Gillian was thirteen, the Commodore selected her from the crowd for a sexual encounter. The Commodore asked Nucky to bring Gillian to him and Nucky complied. The subsequent sexual encounter with an underage girl resulted in Jimmy's conception.

This news changes Jimmy's attitude towards Nucky. He begins to see Nucky in a new light and accepts stories demeaning his character, such as the Commodore's story of how Nucky usurped his power. This new picture of Nucky as a man who should be overthrown begins with an acknowledgment of a specific past wrong. Jimmy already knew about Nucky's other wrongdoings and general shady character prior to hearing Gillian's story. He helped with some of those bad deeds! It's Nucky's role in the rape, however, that makes Jimmy see him as a bad man worth opposing.

Is Nucky's role in the rape itself a genuine moral wrong which Jimmy should oppose? Enabling a rape is certainly a moral wrong. Whether failing to stop the Commodore after presenting Gillian to his employer was a further moral wrong is more debatable, though our intuitions suggest it is. Whether it is a wrong equal to or even greater than the Commodore's wrong is one question. Whether it justifies an alliance with the Commodore is a further question. Given that the harm resulted in Jimmy's birth, whether he's in a position to apportion blame in this case is also worth probing.

Doing, Enabling, and Allowing

The facts of the rape of Gillian Darmody are too incomplete for us to make a full moral analysis. They are only briefly mentioned in a speech in "Paris Green." The Commodore committed a grave moral wrong by sleeping with the thirteen-year-old girl. What Nucky did and what he knew is less clear. Nucky prepared Gillian for the Commodore and did not stop the subsequent sexual act. Is enabling a wrongful act itself a wrongful act? Insofar as Nucky is causally necessary for the rape—he alone would have introduced Gillian to the Commodore—he likely deserves some blame, even if not the same amount as the Commodore.

More knowledge of the Commodore's intentions and more preparation for the act could make Nucky more blameworthy. Is failing to stop the act itself a moral wrong? If Nucky merely introduced the pair and did not know of the Commodore's intentions, but did not stop the Commodore once he gained further knowledge, would we still hold him accountable?

Even granting that Nucky's introduction is a morally wrong act, Jimmy likely knew that Nucky played a role in his mother's seduction from an early age; while he may not have known the details, he was aware of Nucky's relationship with his father. Jimmy was financially and emotionally dependent upon Nucky throughout his childhood, and was therefore not ideally placed to judge Nucky's complicity in the act. An impartial observer can still ask whether Nucky would have committed a moral wrong in a different situation in which he merely allowed the Commodore to meet Gillian rather than introducing them. If Jimmy was in a position to criticize Nucky, should he have done so even if Nucky did not commit an act leading to his mother's seduction?

Many philosophers would hold that Nucky's failure to stop the Commodore may not be wrongful (although they could suggest he committed a wrong earlier). A popular question in moral philosophy concerns whether doing harm is a greater wrong than allowing harm.

A common example comes from the medical ethics literature. Some philosophers maintain that it's wrong to actively hasten the death of a sick individual, participating in "active euthanasia," but it's acceptable to cease treating that individual and allow him or her to die in an act of "passive euthanasia." The basic idea is this: A doctor who stopped treating the Commodore for arsenic poisoning is not as blameworthy as one who gives him further drugs to painlessly end his death. This doctor is certainly not as bad as one who continues to drug him.

Why would this be the case? Philosophers have several explanations. Many appeal to our intuitions about particular cases. These explanations likely won't help Nucky since we think he should have done something to help Gillian. Not introducing her to the Commodore would have been best, but stopping the Commodore later seems like a necessary second-best.

The most straightforward explanations focus on action and inaction. The basic idea is that it's worse to actively cause harm than to fail to act with the result that harm takes place. Whether this saves Nucky in our case is unclear. His act (perhaps indirectly) resulted in harm, but he did not perform the act that directly caused that harm.

Nucky fares better if we focus only on his failure to stop the Commodore if and when he knew the Commodore's intentions. This is an example of inaction. One could plausibly suggest that this inaction is not itself wrong.

Although our feelings about a failure to stop a rape differ from our feelings about allowing an ill person to die, both can be justified on an 'inaction is not wrongful' principle. General hesitancy towards adopted Good Samaritan laws suggests there is some persuasiveness behind these claims in the legal domain. Whether we can be blamed by people other than the state for our inactions is cause for further debate. If not, Nucky may avoid blame altogether. To the extent that we think inaction is wrong, however, it may be worse if it follows wrongful action, such as bringing a child to a predator.

Others try to distinguish doing and allowing harm in other terms, but few (if any) of these distinctions will help Nucky. For instance, malicious intention as a distinguishing feature is arguably not even a genuine distinguishing marker and Nucky's intentions were not known in this case. One can plausibly suggest ill will on his part given what we know about his relationship with the Commodore and his thirst for power. There may be something to be said for the power differential between the Commodore and Nucky, making Nucky less able to assist Gillian, but this alone is likely not enough to make his inaction justifiable.

Regardless of the justification for mere inaction, it's clear that Nucky's involvement in Gillian's rape is slightly more complicated than the euthanasia cases. He did not merely allow the act to take place. Since he introduced Gillian to the Commodore (with possible evil intent), his case *could* be more like one where a doctor gives a patient a harmful drug, then ceases treatment, failing to monitor and respond to the potential harmful effects of the drug.

Depending on how we construct the facts, Nucky arguably committed a wrong earlier and this may give him additional reason to stop the harm from taking place while it is being inflicted. Our intuitions about Nucky suggest that he committed a moral wrong. He not only failed to stop the Commodore, but also enabled the Commodore's wrongful action by introducing him to Gillian. This may make his failure to stop the Commodore worse. Even if we grant both points, we can question whether his wrong is as bad as the Commodore's. Jimmy's actions suggest he may think that it's worse to introduce a young woman to an older man for her violation than it is for the older man to commit that heinous act. At the very least, Jimmy thinks enabling harm is bad enough that it should trigger reassessment of whether he can work with the person who allows it. This reassessment puts Jimmy in league with the man who committed that harm.

Degrees of Blame

Even if we think that both doing and allowing harm are moral wrongs, there is a further question of whether they are equally wrong. To the extent that the Commodore and Nucky both participated in the rape of Gillian Dormady, many would treat both men as moral pariahs, even if the show didn't give us ample other reasons to view them as such. Whether both men are *equally* responsible for the wrong or *equally* deserving of blame is another matter. We may think that allowing harm is a wrong and yet view it as a lesser wrong than committing harm. According to this view, ceasing treatment for a given illness and allowing a patient to die is wrong, but we still think it would be worse if a doctor were to instead hasten death.

Even if we think hastening death can be morally required, we can add malice to the mix to see how directly causing a harm seems more wrongful than allowing it. While this is a debatable reading of issues in health care ethics, I don't defend it so much as I offer it to explain one possible reading of the Gillian Darmody case. The rapist Commodore appears more blameworthy than the young man who enabled him. The Commodore's malice may make him worse than Nucky's subservience, but we would think the Commodore was more blameworthy for his wrongdoing even if Nucky also acted with malice. Jimmy may disagree.

Full knowledge of the circumstances of his conception does not lead Jimmy to treat both the Commodore and Nucky equally. Perhaps oddly, Jimmy's moral censure of Nucky leads him into the Commodore's fold. Once a moral wrong is committed, Jimmy does not seem to recognize that category difference. His actions suggest that he may even view the Commodore as less of a moral monster, but his affiliation appears prompted by familial ties, encouragements from his mother, and acknowledgment of more room for growth in the Commodore's organization rather than bare facts about degrees of responsibility and blameworthiness. Even if one grants that Nucky committed a wrongful act, however, there is reason to question his degree of responsibility.

There are at least two ways of looking at this issue. One focuses on the acting-enabling distinction. It makes sense that everyone should be credited equally for the benefits (or debited for the detriments) of their participation in a collective action. Indeed, Derek Parfit, one of the greatest living philosophers, suggests that such a calculus may be necessary to ensure rational actors participate in morally necessary collective actions. There is, however, ample reason not to apportion *blame* in this manner. Some acts in a causal chain are worse than others, even if the ultimate outcome is very bad. The Commodore's act is worse than Nucky's in this case, even if we want to maintain that both men act monstrously. The second way of looking at this issue focuses on the acting-allowing distinction and holds that action is worse, but this is by no means uncontroversial. If inaction can be a form of action, then inaction can be just as bad.

Regardless of whether either of these arguments allow Nucky to be seen as less morally blameworthy than the Commodore, it's clear that they don't make the Commodore less morally blameworthy. At best, they make both men into moral monsters. It thus seems strange that Jimmy aligns with the Commodore. Jimmy's decisions makes more sense if we remember that this story is not the only thing that causes him to form the alliance. His mother's promptings and other stories about Nucky's wrongful acts towards his family also play a large role. Since this story leads Jimmy to re-evaluate Nucky and hear these stories in a new light, whether his role in Jimmy's conception established Nucky as a wrongdoer is still important, but it does not fully explain Jimmy's actions.

The alliance suggests Nucky was a wrongdoer at that time, even if we want to debate whether he acted as badly as the Commodore. Jimmy can say the Commodore was worse on that day and still say that Nucky's wrongdoing adds to the all-things-considered judgment that he is a worse ally than the Commodore.

Can Jimmy Complain on His Own Behalf?

Can Jimmy really oppose Nucky's action—or inaction? It was necessary for Jimmy's birth after all. While we can recognize Nucky's action as wrong, there is a question as to whether Jimmy should be the one apportioning blame. While Jimmy's life was a difficult one, with incest leading to a war experience that "killed" his original self and replaced it with a man of violence with a wife who does not love him and few enjoyments, it was arguably worth living. We might ask: Who is he to complain?

In one sense, the solution here is easy. Jimmy can believe that Nucky behaved wrongly and apportion blame on his beloved mother's account. This interpretation helps us understand why his mother's suggestions on what Jimmy should do with this knowledge hold such sway. If she (at least seemingly) forgives the Commodore at this moment and wants revenge against Nucky, Jimmy could blame Nucky on her behalf. Whether Jimmy can still blame the Commodore in light of her apparent forgiveness is a further concern, but the beneficiary of a wrongful action can still recognize it as wrongful and continue to blame wrongdoers as long as the victim so blames them.

Jimmy can—and likely should—help the wronged party get restitution. Often, we want such restitution to include giving up the beneficiary's receipts from wrongdoing, but that can't be done here. Jimmy was his mother's pride and joy and she would not want to live without a young man to mold (although Jimmy's son helps her ease the pain when Jimmy eventually dies). Jimmy can know his life is worth living and yet acknowledge it as the result of wrongful action. An attempt to rectify the wrong is an appropriate response thereto. Jimmy can blame others on behalf of his mother.

Whether Jimmy can or should rationally regret the action (or inaction) is another story. At the end of Season Two, Jimmy is prepared for death. He does not guard against what he knows to be an attack on his life, leaving his would-be protector Richard Harrow at home, and walking into a trap. He accepts his death not only to end a conflict, but also partly out of self-interest. He states that he died on the battlefield and welcomes this second death.

Jimmy doesn't seem to think his life is worth living at this point, even if viewers would have liked to continue watching the fan favorite in future seasons. Jimmy's birth was a necessary precursor to that life that wasn't worth living, but the life prior to it was a good one. Jimmy seemed happy at Princeton before punching his teacher. Even after it ceased being good, it seemed worth living. Those goods alone can make his birth good for him. He wouldn't have experienced the goods of his pre-war "death" without it. Some may thus want to conclude that he cannot regret coming into existence.

Philosophers have written a lot about whether we can harm someone by bringing them into the world. The general argument that causing someone to exist can be a harm is that no one is harmed if you fail to bring them into existence, and yet a person who exists is subject to a harm. Not bringing someone into existence does not deprive anyone of anything, while bringing someone into existence always subjects someone to harm. This leads some philosophers to believe that bringing someone into existence can be a harm. Jimmy was exposed to many harms in his life. Whether his life was a net harm is a different concern. If so, he may be able to regret being born.

The philosopher David Benatar believes that it's *always* a harm to cause someone to come into existence. He thus holds that it is immoral to have children and advocates long-term extinction. Since he distinguishes between the morality of causing someone to exist and the morality of ending an existent life, his argument does not suggest that all existent persons should be killed to bring about extinction, but still has the radical result that no new children should be born, entailing the eventual extinction of humanity.

Perhaps Jimmy does not even need to regret being born. We may argue that he could regret being the product of wrongdoing even if he did not regret that he came into existence at all. We understand someone wishing he or she were someone else, untainted by the moral wrong that brought him or her into existence. The problem with this view is that it seems to be a desire for the good of another at the expense of one's self. This may be what Jimmy would choose if he was a God or God-like figure who got to choose what the world would be like, but it wouldn't be in Jimmy's best interest to do so.

If the Commodore and Gillian were not together at least within a reasonably close range of times to the time he was conceived, Jimmy likely wouldn't have been born. Jimmy may think it was good for him that he was born and still regret that the conception ever took place. This position would suggest that it was good for him that he was born, but that it would have been good all things considered if he had not been born. This is not rational egoistic concern, but may be impartially good. It seems to again be based on third-party concerns, like the good of Gillian.

In Season Two, the plan to overthrow Nucky fails. Jimmy eventually aids Nucky in restoring some semblance of order in the later days of the war for control of Atlantic City, but it's too late. Nucky does not forgive Jimmy's betrayal. It was thus ultimately not in Jimmy's interest to turn against Nucky, but he did have reason to view Nucky's role in Gillian's rape as morally wrong and this moral wrongdoing was itself at least one reason to oppose Nucky. His plan's failure does not undermine the fact that he had reason to start it in the first place. His reason had to be based on wrongs to third parties since Jimmy was a beneficiary of that wrongdoing, but it still counts.

8
When It's Right to Lie to a Bootlegger

DON FALLIS

Never let the truth get in the way of a good story.

—ENOCH "NUCKY" THOMPSON

Boardwalk Empire is riddled with deception. At the very outset, Jimmy Darmody, Al Capone, and Billy Winslow create a ruse to hijack a shipment of Arnold Rothstein's whiskey. With his car overturned and blocking the road, Billy pretends to be unconscious and bleeding. When Rothstein's men stop to investigate, Jimmy and Al come out of the woods with rifles and end up shooting all of them. Subsequently, Nucky's organization employs all sorts of deceit to cover up this crime. In fact, during Prohibition, the whiskey itself, which is diluted and sold with fake labels, is designed to deceive.

Jimmy, Al, and Billy fool Rothstein's men by making it look as if there has been a car accident. But most of the denizens of Atlantic City deceive by actually telling *lies*. For instance, as part of the cover-up, Agent Eric Sebso kills Billy in cold blood to keep him from testifying, but he tells his superiors in the Department of Internal Revenue that it was self-defense. Jimmy and Sheriff Elias "Eli" Thompson tell their partners that the Commodore is fine when he has actually been incapacitated by a stroke.

The Italian-American gangster Johnny Torrio lies to the Irish-American gangster Charlie Sheridan about just

wanting to have a "meet" to discuss dividing up Chicago's
Greektown neighborhood. (In fact, the plan is to slaughter
Sheridan and his entire gang using guns that Jimmy and Al
have hidden with the coat-check girl.) Unlike most other
bootleggers, Rothstein does not attempt to deceive people
about the quality of his whiskey. He only sells "the best
scotch from Britain" ("Belle Femme"). But he does lie about
his involvement in fixing the 1919 World Series.

And Nucky Thompson himself lies to other bootleggers,
to other politicians, to the honest citizens of Atlantic City, to
his wife—in other words, to just about everybody—about just
about everything. Perhaps the most glaring example of
Nucky's duplicity comes at the beginning of Season Two
("21"). After the Ku Klux Klan shoots up Albert "Chalky"
White's liquor warehouse, Nucky tells the congregation of
the black church that he will not rest "until these hooded
cowards are brought to justice." Then the scene cuts to the
white church where Nucky is telling the congregation the
exact opposite. He promises to teach these "coloreds" a lesson
with "an iron fist."

As the Commodore points out to Jimmy, Nucky's a "manipulative son of a bitch" ("A Return to Normalcy"). Of
course, the Commodore himself is nothing to write home
about. As Nucky tells Jimmy, "your father is a very duplicitous man" ("21").

Just Give Me the Straight Dope

Most philosophers think that it's usually wrong to lie and deceive. In fact, a few philosophers, such as Immanuel Kant in
his essay "On a Supposed Right to Lie from Altruistic Motives,"
and Saint Augustine in his *De Mendacio*, go so far as to claim
that lying is *always* wrong. Here's how extreme their view is:
imagine that you are hiding a Jewish family in your home during the Nazi Occupation. An SS officer knocks on your door and
asks if any Jews are living at this residence. Even if it is the
only way to save your friends from being murdered, Kant says
that "it would be a crime to lie to a murderer."

Now, Kant's complete ban on lying surely goes too far. Even if it's usually wrong to lie, there are going to be some exceptions. At the very least, as the Dutch philosopher Hugo Grotius suggests in his book *Law of War and Peace*, it must be "permissible to say what is false when we are unable in any other way to save the life of an innocent person." However, the lies in *Boardwalk Empire* cannot be defended on the grounds that they're necessary in order to save lives. In fact, it's quite the opposite. A large number of these lies lead to somebody getting killed. Most notably, when Nucky tricks Jimmy into coming to the War Memorial alone in the dead of night, it does not end well for Jimmy.

There is really no question that much of the lying in *Boardwalk Empire* is morally wrong. After all, the lies are typically told for selfish—and often nefarious—purposes. Also, they are intended to deceive honest citizens—such as churchgoers—who would like to know the truth and arguably have a right to it.

However, quite a few of the lies told in *Boardwalk Empire* lack one or more of these prototypical features of lies. First, not all of them are told for selfish purposes. For instance, Margaret Schroeder lies to Nucky in an attempt to help her former employer, Madame Jeunet. Unless Nucky reduces Jeunet's protection payments, her dress shop, *La Belle Femme*, will go out of business. In order to get him to do this, Margaret tells him that Jeunet is the only person that she trusts to make her "look pretty" ("Belle Femme").

Second, not all of the lies in *Boardwalk Empire* are told to people who want to know the truth. Many of them are told to people who—at least deep down—want to be deceived. According to the Great Hardeen—brother of Harry Houdini and founder of the Magicians Guild, "deception requires complicity, however subconscious" ("Paris Green").

Third, many of the lies are told to bootleggers and gangsters who—being inveterate liars themselves—probably don't deserve the truth. For instance, Nucky and Jimmy are frequently the victims as well as the perpetrators of lies. In addition, since Agent Nelson Van Alden lies to the prohibition agents that work for him, to his superiors, and to his wife, it is difficult to sympathize when witnesses and suspects lie to him.

Finally, several of the lies are not even intended to deceive. For instance, when questioned about his whereabouts on the night of the hijacking, Jimmy tells Agent Van Alden, "I went to the movies. I fell asleep. I got up. I walked home. I went to bed. You want to charge me. Charge me. I got nothing else to say" ("Belle Femme"). Jimmy does not expect Van Alden to believe him. He just needs to stick to his alibi in order to keep from getting charged with five murders.

Given their unusual properties, you might be tempted to think that some of these lies could be justified or at least excused. Admittedly, none of these lies are told to save lives. But what could be so wrong with lying to help someone, lying to someone who wants to be deceived, lying to a liar, or lying without the intent to deceive? In order to see why these lies aren't justified, we first need to look at *exactly why* lying is wrong when it is wrong.

Taking the Decision Out of My Hands

The main reason that lying is wrong is that it harms the person who is lied to. When we trust someone who lies to us, we end up with a false belief about the world. And false beliefs can often lead to bad decisions. In other words, we're likely to decide to do something that we wouldn't have done if we knew the truth. For instance, the ward bosses who defected from Nucky's organization to the Commodore's organization would have switched sides again if they had known that the Commodore "can't even take a piss by himself" ("Gimcrack & Bunkum"). In a similar vein, Supervisor Frederick Elliot wouldn't have kept Sebso on the job if he knew that Sebso was killing witnesses on behalf of bootleggers. (But if Elliot had figured out what Sebso was up to, he would probably have just arrested Sebso rather than drowning him as Van Alden does.) And Sheridan would never have sat down with Torrio if he knew that the meet was really a set-up.

Bad decisions can certainly lead to dire consequences. In fact, in Atlantic City, someone who is deceived often ends up dead. But Kant and many other philosophers emphasize that people are always *directly* harmed by lies. The liar violates the *autonomy* of the person who is lied to. By manipulating the information that this person has access to, the liar takes away her ability to make informed choices about what to do and about what to believe. The propaganda produced by early temperance activists provides a good example of this.

As is illustrated nicely by Burns and Novick's *Prohibition* (Florentine Films, 2011), alcohol consumption was a serious social problem in the late nineteenth and early twentieth centuries. Despite what he tells the Women's Temperance League of Atlantic City, Nucky did not, as a child, have to go out into a blizzard and kill wharf rats in order feed his family. But many children would go hungry because their father would drink up the paycheck at the local watering hole. So, in order to deter people from drinking alcohol, the Women's Christian Temperance Union created "texts filled with lurid misinformation calculated to terrify. Just one drink, some books alleged, could burn away the lining of the throat and stomach and begin eating away at the liver and kidneys. . . . and always, some textbooks warned, there was the fearful possibility that drinking could spark spontaneous combustion, bursting suddenly into fatal blue flame" ("A Nation of Drunkards," *Prohibition*). Now, even if you believe these lies, you can still choose to take a drink. But if you think that you're likely to die from one sip, there's an important sense in which the choice has really been taken out of your hands.

After the Stunt You Pulled, You Don't Trust Me?

Lying is not just wrong because it harms the person who is lied to. As the American essayist Ralph Waldo Emerson put it, "every violation of truth is not only a sort of suicide in the liar, but is a stab at the health of human society." The problem is that lies tend to make us all less trusting. (At least,

they tend to make us less trusting if the deception is ultimately revealed as it usually is in *Boardwalk Empire*.)

Trust is an extremely important and valuable commodity.
Someone can certainly go off to the Pine Barrens and try to
fend completely for herself. However, in order to survive and
prosper in the world, people usually choose to make all sorts
of co-operative arrangements with each other. It's clear from
Boardwalk Empire that this applies to criminals as well as
to honest citizens. Working together in a temperance league
or in a bootlegging operation requires trust. If we can't rely
on what other people tell us, it's very difficult to co-operate
effectively. For instance, we have to keep checking that people are actually doing what they say that they will do.

When someone lies to us, she betrays our trust. So, when
we find out that she lied to us, it is much more difficult to
trust this person going forward. In fact, it is likely to make
us less trusting in general. In *Boardwalk Empire*, many of
the people whose trust is betrayed end up dead. So, like
Charlie Sheridan, they are no longer around to be untrust-
ing. However, everyone else who is aware of what went down
is less trusting going forward. After Jimmy tries unsuccessfully to make a deal selling liquor to Rothstein, Charles
"Lucky" Luciano invites Jimmy to meet with him and Meyer
Lansky. Since he knows first-hand how these things go,
Jimmy is understandably skeptical. He thinks that Lucky
takes him for a "simp" and that it's probably a "set-up" ("Ourselves Alone"). So, he initially refuses the invitation.

Lying is not the only form of deception that can harm people and that can diminish trust. For instance, when Jimmy
finally catches up with Liam—the member of Sheridan's
gang who slashed his girlfriend's face, he says, "Relax. I'm
not going to kill you" ("Home"). Although this statement is,
strictly speaking, true, it suggests falsely that Liam is not in
any immediate danger. So, Liam is a sitting target for
Jimmy's new friend Richard Harrow to shoot him in the head
with a rifle from across the street. But since there are plenty
of *outright lies*—that is, statements that are actually false,
or that are at least believed by the speaker to be false—to

keep us busy, I won't worry about statements that are merely misleading. Now that we have a better grip on why it's wrong to lie in general, let's look more carefully at some of those *out-of-the-ordinary* outright lies from *Boardwalk Empire*.

Lying to Help Others

Not many altruistic lies are told in Atlantic City. But at least a few lies are intended to help others. Most of these lies are told by Margaret. In addition to lying to help Madame Jeunet, she lies to help Nucky. After Nucky is arrested for election fraud, she goes on her own initiative to Nucky's office dressed up as a destitute woman who is seeking Nucky's help. By claiming to be unwell and needing to use the facilities, she is able to retrieve Nucky's ledger and several thousand dollars in cash before the State's Attorney is able to find it. Also, when Emily is frightened by the fact that she can't move her legs, Margaret says, "it's nothing at all" even though she knows otherwise.

Another example of altruistic lying is when Prohibition agents lie in order to protect the interests of society. Admittedly, Van Alden's lies are typically self-interested. He tries to hide the fact that he is living with a former cabaret dancer who is carrying his child and he tries to keep secret what really happened to Sebso. But in real life, Prohibition agents sometimes did lie in order to catch bootleggers. On the opposite side of the country from Atlantic City, Roy Olmstead (formerly a Seattle Police lieutenant) was the most successful bootlegger in the Northwest. In 1924, William Whitney, Assistant Prohibition Director for Washington State, and sixteen Prohibition agents armed with shotguns entered Olmstead's home. They "took over the telephone, pretending to be the Olmsteads, Whitney and his wife then made call after call to Olmstead's accomplices, asking them to bring whisky to his house right away, as each one arrived he was arrested" ("A Nation of Scofflaws," *Prohibition*).

However, the fact that something is intended to do good does not show that it *is* good. As Harvard philosopher Sissela

Bok points out in her book *Lying: Moral Choice in Public and Private Life*, altruistic liars are often mistaken about whether the benefits of lying actually outweigh the costs. For one thing, there are often benefits *to the liar* that create an unconscious bias in favor of lying. After all, Margaret would lose her comfortable life if Nucky's ledger were used to convict him. Even her lie to help Madame Jeunet turns out not to be so altruistic. When Jeunet offers her a dress for Emily, Margaret replies, "My daughter didn't help you Madame Jeunet. I did," and we next see her out on the town wearing an expensive dress that she says is a "gift from Madame Jeunet" ("Belle Femme"). Furthermore, when people see themselves as trying to do good, they often ignore the fact that even altruistic lies—including Margaret's "white lie" to her daughter—can potentially diminish trust.

Lying to the Easily Bamboozled

Quite a few of the *honest* citizens of Atlantic City are quite credulous. When Pete—one of the two hunters that Richard meets in the woods—claims to have once seen a flying horse in Atlantic City, his friend Glenmore notes that Pete's "an easily bamboozled individual" ("Gimcrack & Bunkum"). After Jimmy says that a newspaper story about Jack Dempsey is "baloney," his wife Angela tells him that "they couldn't write it if it wasn't true" ("Boardwalk Empire"). In real life, Capone took advantage of such credulity by giving money to reporters in an attempt to manage his public image. According to Jack Clarke ("Mayor Richard J. Daley's personal gumshoe"), "Capone's idea was that, everybody reads the newspaper, and most people are stupid enough to believe what's written in the newspapers" ("A Nation of Hypocrites," *Prohibition*).

In the early 1920s, many people believed newspaper reports that one of Tsar Nicholas's daughters had miraculously survived the Bolshevik Revolution. However, as Margaret's cynical neighbor Edith Mauer probably could have predicted, the young woman suffering from amnesia after being rescued from a suicide attempt in Berlin was not really the Grand Duchess Anastasia of Russia. It is almost as if the people of Atlantic City are asking to be deceived. Even the members of the two church congregations—at least to some degree—allow themselves to be fooled. Nucky is just telling them what they want to hear. What could be wrong with giving them what they want?

Nevertheless, lying to gullible people *is* wrong. Although they might want—at some level—to be deceived, they have not given anybody permission to deceive them. When we attend a magic show or when we sit down at the poker table, we do consent to being deceived. Thus, there is nothing wrong with deception in these contexts. After his opponent folds and says, "Take it. I was bluffing," Rothstein replies, "I know. So was I" ("Broadway Limited"). While the opponent is not happy about being fooled, he cannot legitimately complain that Rothstein did anything morally wrong. Bluffing at the poker table is not going to diminish trust beyond the poker table. But falsely claiming to be a lost princess is.

Some philosophers, such as Albert Z. Carr in his essay "Is Business Bluffing Ethical?" suggest that business is just like a poker game. This would mean that, if you go into the bootlegging business, you *have* given your consent to having other people try to deceive you. But even if this is right, there are often still reasons not to lie to a lying bootlegger.

Admittedly, credulous people are often partially responsible for being duped. But this does not mean that the person who lies to them bears any less responsibility. In a similar vein, Hans Schroeder's own actions—such as beating up his wife and getting in Nucky's face at the casino—certainly led to his being killed. But that doesn't mean that Nucky and Eli are not morally responsible for beating the man to death.

Lying to Liars

Many of the people who are lied to in *Boardwalk Empire* are liars themselves. Does the fact that they are liars make it okay for someone else to lie to them? According to the British philosopher Jonathan Dancy (on *Philosophy Bites*), "some-body who is a habitual liar deserves lies. I don't see that what you are doing when you lie to them is to some extent wrong because it's a lie. . . . This is absolutely the right way to treat such a person." While this seems plausible, what's the argument?

It might be suggested that lying to a liar is a special case of lying to someone who has no right to the truth. Given his murderous intentions, the SS officer clearly does not have a moral right to know whether any Jews are staying at your residence. Grotius plausibly claims that it is not wrong to lie to such people. In a similar vein, it might be suggested that it is not wrong to lie to prevaricating bootleggers because they don't have a right to the truth either.

However, there are a couple of problems with this line of argument. First, the fact that you have lied to someone on some topic does not necessarily mean that you don't have a right to the truth from someone else on some other topic. For instance, while Nucky and Jimmy lie to other gangsters, and to each other, about their criminal activities, it's not clear that they therefore do not have a right to know that their wives are cheating on them.

Second, the fact that someone has no right to the truth only means that we have no obligation to provide her with the truth. It does not mean that it is permissible to *lie* to her. In some cases, lying may be the only way to keep the truth from someone. For instance, when the investors ask about the Com-modore's health, Jimmy says, "my father is fine" ("Gimcrack & Bunkum"). Similarly, Eli tells Alderman George O'Neill, "I saw him this morning. We had breakfast. Eggs. Bacon. The man loves his bacon." If Jimmy and Eli had not said anything, these people would likely have drawn the conclusion that there was a problem with the Commodore. But most people in *Boardwalk Empire* could withhold the truth just by keeping their mouths shut. They lie because it is important that some-one have a false belief and not just lack a true belief.

Sometimes people try to justify lying to a liar on the grounds that it teaches the liar a lesson. But as Bok points out, it is not clear that the lesson it teaches is that he should-n't lie. Instead, he might just learn that he should lie since everybody else does. That is the lesson that most people in *Boardwalk Empire* seem to have learned. The only person who has any second thoughts about lying is Margaret: "I've stolen, and cheated, and deceived, and now I'm being pun-ished for those sins as are the ones I love" ("Under God's Power She Flourishes").

Admittedly, a liar himself really may have no grounds for complaining about being lied to. But that doesn't mean that lying to him is a good thing to do. As the old saying goes, two wrongs don't make a right. Moreover, even if we need not worry about how lying to a liar harms him, it's still the case that lying to a liar can diminish trust which harms all of us. As Kant puts it in his *Lectures on Ethics*, "whoever may have told me a lie, I do him no wrong if I lie to him in return, but I violate the right of mankind; for I have acted contrary to the condition, and the means, under which a society of men can come about, and thus contrary to the right of humanity."

Bald-Faced Lying

Not every false statement is a lie. After failing to convince O'Neill that the Commodore is fine, Eli kills him with a wrench and gets Deputy Ray Halloran to help him move the body.

HALLORAN: Jesus! Is it somebody I know?

ELI: It's Mary Pickford.

HALLORAN: You killed Mary Pickford? ("Gimcrack & Bunkum")

Even though he didn't really kill "America's Sweetheart," Eli is clearly not lying. It's just a joke.

But a false statement can be a lie even if it is not intended to deceive. As long as false statements are made seriously rather than ironically, they are what Roy Sorensen calls "Bald-Faced Lies!" Unlike Eli, Jimmy is not joking when he says that he was at the movies rather than out in the woods shooting people. Similarly, even though he doesn't expect Nucky to believe him, Rothstein claims with a straight face that he won $93,000 at the casino simply because he is "a skilled player" ("Boardwalk Empire"). But even if they are lies, what could be the problem with them if no one is going to be deceived?

It can't be that bald-faced lies are wrong because they create false beliefs that lead to bad decisions. Jimmy's lie does not convince Van Alden that he is innocent and Rothstein's lie does not convince Nucky that he is not cheating. Also, bald-faced lies cannot be wrong because they diminish trust. As Sorensen points out, "bald-faced lies do not fool anyone. They are no more a threat to truth telling than sarcastic remarks." Thus, Sorensen concludes that bald-faced lies are "morally-neutral." In other words, while it might be very annoying for Jimmy to persist in saying things that he and Van Alden both know to be false, it is not morally wrong according to Sorensen.

However, contrary to what Sorensen claims, bald-faced lies—at least some of them—are wrong and they are wrong for one of the main reasons that deceptive lies are wrong. Deceptive lies attempt to get people to act in certain ways—often against their own interests—by getting them to acquire false beliefs. But the false beliefs are only a means to an end. Bald-faced lies simply attempt to get people to act in certain ways by other means. Bald-faced lies typically make it socially awkward for people not to act in the way that the speaker wants. Thus, even though it does not deceive, a bald-faced lie can still violate the autonomy of the person who is lied to.

Admittedly, it is not clear that Jimmy's lie is manipulative. Van Alden cannot charge Jimmy with the murders simply because he does not have enough evidence. Since we have a right against self-incrimination in this country, Jimmy could've just kept his mouth shut. However, Rothstein's lie *is* somewhat manipulative. It is socially awkward—and often dangerous to your health—to call someone a cheater to his face. And, given who Rothstein is, it is even more difficult to call *him* a cheater. (As the casino manager Lolly Steinman says, "I don't wanna say nothing. But this Rothstein's a cheater. Honestly, if he wasn't who he is, they'd've found him in the fuckin' alley.") But Rothstein's lie raises the stakes further on Nucky. In order to do anything other than simply write-off the loss, Nucky would now have to call him a liar as well as a cheat.

Is There an Honest Man in Atlantic City?

After Nucky is charged with "election rigging," a reporter asks him, "Is there an honest man in Atlantic City?" to which Nucky responds, "Is there a sober reporter at the *Philadelphia Inquirer*?" ("Ourselves Alone"). But the reporter is right. Atlantic City is full of liars. However, not all of their lies are intended to deceive people who would like to know the truth and who arguably have a right to it. In fact, a few of them are intended to help others. As a result, some of their lies might not be as morally wrong as they could be. But even so, Nucky and rest of the gang are still behaving badly whenever they lie.[1]

---

[1] I would like to thank Tony Doyle, Richard Greene, James Mahon, Kay Mathiesen, and Dan Zelinski for many helpful suggestions.

Part III

Fortified Wines

9
Nucky Cleans Up

WIELAND SCHWANEBECK

When it comes to personal hygiene, you've got to hand it to Uncle Nucky—the man is thorough! Although *Boardwalk Empire* teaches us time and again that booze-trafficking is a dirty business and that it's very hard to keep your hands clean (not to mention your shirt, which is likely to catch bloodstains), Nucky Thompson usually manages to look spick and span and to cut a dashing figure. He even reminds Margaret's kids of the importance of personal hygiene by reciting a little poem:

> There are germs of every kind
> in every food that you will find,
> in the market or upon the bill of fare.
> Drinking water's just as risky
> as the so-called deadly whiskey,
> and it's often a mistake to breathe the air. ("Home")

Then again, we might ask ourselves whether Nucky, though he may look immaculate, is really the most suitable teacher to give lessons to Emily and Theodore. It is, after all, in Nucky's house where Emily contracts Polio, in spite of his poetic lessons, and Nucky also plays a major role in providing Atlantic City with what the Women's Temperance Union sees as the major poison threatening American health: "Liquor, thy name's delirium!"

Occasionally, Nucky's insistence on cleanliness clashes with the dirty business he gets entangled in. Nowhere does this become more evident than when he explains his personal policy: "One hand washes the other and both hands wash the face" ("Anastasia"). This raises the question of whether it's really possible to remain free of germs and bacilli when you're not quite sure where that other hand has been before, and whether the hygienic issues affecting some of Atlantic City's inhabitants don't indicate threats to the American nation at large. For Nucky's lessons on hygiene and his struggle with the temperance movement show an ancient philosophical concept in practice: the idea of the body politic and the various threats leveled against it.

The Body Politic and Its Various Parts

The idea of referring to the nation and its sovereign by using the image of the body dates back to ancient philosophy. Nowadays, expressions such as *head* of state or *member* of parliament seem so self-explanatory that they've become so-called dead metaphors, that is: metaphors which are used so often that we don't recognize them as metaphors anymore.

Some of the earliest written records of the body politic date back to Ancient Rome. Cicero (106–43 B.C.) talks about the body politic in some of his letters and in his defense of the consul Lucius Licinius Murena (*Pro Murena*). The philosopher Seneca (4 B.C.–A.D. 65), on the other hand, whose work mainly dealt with moral issues, used the body politic image in order to teach the future emperor Nero (37–68) a thing or two about virtue. Since Nero enjoyed a reputation for having a bit of a temper, Seneca was well-advised to write a little essay called *De Clementia*, reminding his boss of the importance of showing mercy—Nucky Thompson, who knows the value of a good book, might own a copy, though he probably doesn't consult it very often.

De Clementia has its roots in Seneca's Stoic philosophy, and he argues that the emperor and the state both depend on each other. To make this a little clearer, he uses the image of head and body (though he sometimes talks about the mind, too) to refer to political entities. According to Seneca, the mind (meaning the sovereign ruler) may be powerful, and it may be in charge of the whole operation, but we must not forget that it's also quite fragile: the mind's location is far from certain, and since it is "hidden and tiny," it requires help to get around—"hands, feet and eyes do its business"—and a skin to protect it (*De Clementia*, I.3.5).

And so, Seneca argues, mind and body depend on each other, and "neither could be separated without the ruin of the other" (I.4.3). Remembering the importance of the people is a lesson which the emperors in Ancient Rome probably were in dire need of, for back then it would not just have been the Women's Temperance Union and Chalky White's army of African-American low-wage workers struggling to gain political power—the majority of people had no way of influencing political decisions.

During the following centuries, philosophers continued to use the image of the body politic in their writings, even more so in the early modern period, where new scientific discoveries about human anatomy allowed for the analogy to be extended. An English doctor named William Harvey (1578–1657) discovered the principles of blood circulation, and it was about the same time that politicians started talking about problems in the national blood supply whenever they wanted to raise taxes. When they tried to warn the people of foreign invaders, they talked about a threat to the intestinal tract of the nation.

In Shakespeare's plays, written around the same time, different strata of society are repeatedly described as parts of the body—he likens the aristocracy to the belly of the nation and the peasants to its feet, for example. Theoretically, each part of the body politic could contract a lethal disease, so the welfare of the whole body had to be guaranteed by keeping the individual parts in good health. Nucky is an expert on that—he knows everyone in Atlantic City by name and values the importance of every member in his organization.

If we were to take Nucky's emphatic advice to "read a fucking book" on occasion ("Pilot"), and went through all the various political treatises published during the Elizabethan Age and after, we would come across a great number of different examples of this metaphor, and we would find that the body politic doesn't just have a head and a pair of feet, but also all the necessary vital organs, a nervous system, a nose, a belly, eyes and ears. If the body politic is missing one thing, it is genitals—there are no references to its penis and testicles in the relevant sources (needless to say that the female anatomy is completely ignored—the Elizabethan Age may have been dominated by a female ruler, but even she was careful not to draw attention to her biological sex, so as not to appear weak).

Although kings were expected to show off their potency and their various mistresses, the people seem to have preferred to think of their sovereigns as men of the mind and from whose head, according to Seneca, health is expected to spring, "according to the vitality or faintness of the soul" (II.2.1). The most famous illustration of this idea is probably the title-page of *Leviathan*, a famous book by the English philosopher Thomas Hobbes (1588–1679), in which he lays down his political theory. It shows the state as a muscular, bearded figure carrying a crown, a crosier and a sword—a decidedly masculine representation of the body politic. However, even the mighty Leviathan prefers not to show off his manhood, cowering behind the landscape that he is ruling over.

Temperance and the Body Politic in *Boardwalk Empire*

If we think of the 1920s politicians in *Boardwalk* as the legitimate successors of kings—for it is still the rulers of the state who give their faces to the body politic, no matter what the political system—then we get an idea why they are always so eager to avoid scandal and to enjoy themselves behind closed doors, where no-one will see them get drunk, eat oysters, or worse. Nucky usually talks about showing his friends "a good time," which entails getting wasted and sleeping with prostitutes—Kessler, the helpful Hun, knows what his boss's visitors are interested in: "You vant *Schlampen, ja?*" Indeed they do. No matter if it's the young hotshot lawyer from New York or President Warren Harding, who preaches stability and so-called American values, but produces a child out of wedlock—there isn't one political player in *Boardwalk Empire* who doesn't come across as a boozing, fun-loving, and hedonistic creature.

Officially, they are guardians of the moral order, for in order to gain respect as a political leader, it seems an unspoken agreement that you don't give in to your baser needs. That's why Nucky's only advice to Ed Bader, the future mayor of Atlantic City, is to have "a strong arm and clean record" ("Paris Green"). In this respect, we don't seem to have come that far since antiquity, as politicians still resign over private affairs, which are not related to their political activities, but shatter the image they have built for themselves. The idea of an abstinent, clean national body does not go well with the way real politics are done in *Boardwalk*, and boy, is it a dirty business! Power talks happen over drinks, connections are made in the brothels of Chicago and Atlantic City, and whilst shaking hands with suffragettes, priests, and war heroes is all nice and well, the real political business is done behind closed doors, ties loosened, cigars in hand, half-naked girls running about.

Thus demystified, the figure of the politician appears as a human being, made of flesh and blood, treating himself to everything which public demands will forbid him. We like our politicians clean-shaven and immaculate, because they are representatives of the state and we like to think of the state as clean and immaculate, too. As vices go in *Boardwalk Empire*, boozing is on the harmless side. Enemies are wiped out so mercilessly that the blood sometimes threatens to come straight at the viewer (aren't you glad that Big Jim Colosimo's death wasn't in 3D?), and Nucky is usually busy entertaining his visitors or plotting revenge rather than addressing his voters' concerns or teaching Emily and Theodore about hygiene.

This theme plays a prominent role throughout the whole show and it is emphasized by the historical background: *Boardwalk Empire* shows that Prohibition was very much an attempt to keep the body politic clean by preventing allegedly poisonous substances from entering its system. When the Women's Temperance Union and other groups such as the Anti-Saloon League set out to make people aware of the dangers of alcohol, they tried to cure a whole nation of what they saw as a disease, and the effects of whiskey and beer were not just regarded as an attack on the liver of the state, but as a danger to its various other parts, too. The argument went that alcohol not only destroyed families, but also threatened the economic system—an alcoholic isn't worth a lot in terms of bringing up his children, looking after his wife or doing his job properly. According to a 1910 sermon by the Reverend Charles F. Aked, the drunkard was moreover to be seen as dangerous "because he has temporarily lost all cognizance of law, of duty, of decency, and of regard to his fellow-men."[1]

It took some time before this view became more widespread in the United States, though. World War I was a landmark event in that respect, for it allowed the supporters of the temperance movement to argue that the body of the nation was directly threatened by alcohol—after all, what good is a soldier who has been fed a diet of Scotch and beer? The French allies were seen as unreliable, because they consumed too much red wine and were allegedly unable to provide their American fellows with pure drinking water.[2] In addition, American soldiers were expected to keep themselves clean, and the fear of unknown germs they might bring back from overseas became the subject of campaigns.

When Jimmy returns home from the trenches in Europe and is examined by a doctor, a contemporary propaganda

---

[1] Rev. Charles F. Aked, D.D., and His Divine Master, "A Contrast," in *Prohibition: Its Relation to Temperance, Good Morals and Sound Government*, edited by Joseph Debar (Cincinnati, 1910), p. 57.

[2] Daniel Okrent, *Last Call: The Rise and Fall of Prohibition* (Scribner's, 2010), p. 98.

poster can be spotted on the clinic walls ("Home"). It shows a warning to the GIs typical of the time: "You kept fit and defeated the Hun. Now set a high standard for a clean America! Stamp out venereal diseases" ("Home"). Again, the body politic—and, by implication, the nation—seems under attack where sexual matters arise. So if booze and whores represent a danger to the American nation, and if, to quote again from the poem Nucky recites for the children, "every microbe and bacillus / has a different way to kill us, / and in time will claim us for their own," then surely abstinence must be the best option. Right?

Why "No Alcohol!" Is No Solution

Not quite, according to the action in *Boardwalk*. And not just because the members of the Temperance Union don't exactly look like they're a whole bunch of fun. The viewer is not only shown that politicians and spin-doctors like Nucky himself are hypocrites who lie, steal, cheat, get their hands dirty, and give a completely false impression of themselves, but also that purity and cleanliness are an illusion. It's saying something that amongst the various groups who populate 1920s Atlantic City, the group that most fiercely struggles to purify the national body of America is the Ku Klux Klan, whose fight for "Purity and Sobriety" takes radical and inhumane steps, such as the massacre amongst Chalky White's men ("21").

Another character on the show who tries to do his part in clearing or ridding the body politic of foul elements is Agent Nelson Van Alden, an upright defender of the nation—that is, until he gets Nucky's former mistress Lucy pregnant, kills his own colleague, embezzles money from the bureau, and joins the Chicago racket. This man is so taken with the idea of personal hygiene that he's repeatedly shown washing his hands, explicitly refers to the toilet as a water-closet, and when he pens a letter to his wife (who bears an uncanny resemblance to the spinster depicted in Grant Wood's famous painting, *American Gothic*), it is not to tell her how much he misses her, but to remind her to regularly run the faucets ("The Ivory Tower").

Their reproductive problems also suggest that the future of America may not be in the hands of these hygiene fanatics who are obsessed with the idea of purifying mind and body. Van Alden's killing of his corrupt partner, Agent Sebso, is a particularly grim lesson in cleanliness (and one which we're glad Nucky doesn't apply to Margaret's kids). When Van Alden drowns Sebso in front of a horrified African-American Baptist community, he repeatedly shouts, "Let these waters wash you clean!" ("Paris Green").

The teetotalers are clearly not to be trusted—either they are full-blown nut-jobs like Van Alden, or cold-blooded psychopaths with methods to rival those of Nucky, like Arnold Rothstein, who is incidentally as dedicatedly a drinker of buttermilk as Van Alden. In *Boardwalk Empire*, the traditional idealized image of a pure, healthy national body turns out to be an illusion, and we're shown that the body politic is of a much more ambiguous nature than traditional political philosophy would have it. Temperance may have avid supporters like Mrs. McGarry, but *Boardwalk* does not provide any memorable role models who would show it to be a remedy to cure America of its major diseases, such as, for instance, organized crime.

What it does provide is a whiskey-loving main character so slick that he never appears unshaven throughout the whole first season. Nucky's first proper crisis in Season Two goes hand in hand with his not only running out of shaving soap ("What Does the Bee Do?"), but also with accidentally cutting himself whilst shaving ("Ourselves Alone"). When Nucky suffers, so does his usually immaculate appearance.

Nucky Thompson is often shown as he prepares for his public appearances: a boy scout getting ready for his Sunday outing to church. He has his shoes shined, puts a carnation into his buttonhole, dons one of his many suits, and throws a tantrum when Lucy denies him access to the bathroom or when the silver spoons aren't shiny. But although Nucky's first appearance in the show sees him addressing the women of the Temperance League, recounting a heart-warming (but, needless to say, totally made-up) story about the dangers of alcohol, and concluding that "Prohibition means progress," he is certainly not the poster boy for this slogan. When they chose Nucky's surname, the creators of the show even played a joke on the founding fathers (or rather *mothers*) of the temperance movement, for whilst Nucky is modeled on Atlantic City's famous treasurer, Enoch Johnson, he bears the surname of Eliza Thompson ("Mother Thompson"), whose activities proved the starting point for the temperance movement in the late nineteenth century.

As the credit sequence of the show makes clear, Nucky is literally standing in an ocean of booze, and his criminal activities—bootlegging, gambling, and pimping amongst them—are hard to keep track of. But what else would we expect from the casting of Steve Buscemi, an actor whose former credits include the sleazy kidnapper Carl in the Coen Brothers' *Fargo* (1995) and Randall the chameleon in *Monsters, Inc.* (2001), in the role of an Irish-American? Nucky himself tells us what an Irishman who doesn't drink would be called—"a corpse" ("Nights in Ballygran").

So how does he get away with it—preaching the need for a purified national body, one who is perfectly in line with ancient thought by abstaining from alcohol and denying his own sexuality, while at the same time practicing the very vices a political leader must officially condemn? Nucky himself tells us how it's done right in the first episode: "First rule of politics, kiddo: Never let the truth get in the way of a good story" ("Pilot"). Nucky thus indirectly admits where he got his political training, and it's certainly not the school of Seneca, but the most (in)famous guide to politics in the early modern period, Niccolò Macchiavelli's *The Prince* (1513). Machiavelli stresses that the major discipline for the ruler is the art of war, and that a successful politician does not necessarily have to possess good qualities, "but it is very necessary to appear to have them. And I shall dare to say this also, that to have them and always to appear to have them is useful; to appear merciful, faithful, humane, religious, upright, and to be so, but with a mind so framed that should you require not to be so, you may be able and know how to change to the opposite." So where Seneca argued that the body politic must be governed by a head of state who *is* clement, Machiavelli emphasizes that the ruler should *appear* clement, above all.

In other words: Get your hands dirty whichever way you like, but remember to wash them before waving to the press. Nucky gets some sort of comeuppance in "Peg of Old," when an assassin hired by Jimmy nearly kills him, hitting Nucky's right hand (the one reserved for handshakes) instead, but he usually has the last laugh. Like most of the other scheming, dubious politicians, and power-players who appear on the show, he reminds the viewers of Pontius Pilate, who likewise considered washing his hands sufficient proof of his innocence. Then again, Pilate didn't exactly go down in history for making a whole lot of sensible decisions during his time in public office, either.

The King Is Dead, Long Live the Kingpin!

So far, we've skipped one crucial point: Does it make sense to view Nucky and his fellow gangsters and politicians in the tradition of ancient emperors and medieval kings who decided the nation's fate and whom the body politic metaphor applied to in the first place?

Kings are most frequently cited in discussions of the body politic: not only do they act as heads of state, but they are themselves expected to represent an indivisible unit of two bodies, their (mortal) natural body on the one hand, and their (immortal) body politic on the other. Can this ancient idea be linked to 1920s Atlantic City, or even to our day and age? By all means, yes! We may have come a long way since Seneca or Cicero, but the political changes that have occurred since the days of Ancient Rome have not done away with the idea of looking at the state as an organic whole, an entity that depends on the smooth interaction of its individual parts. Neither have we ceased to be taken with the idea of purity—we want our politicians to be clean and unadulterated.

In this respect, there's a thread running from the Roman Empire to the democracy of the United States. For Van Alden, Atlantic City has a lot in common with the vanished city of Carthage by the Sea ("Return to Normalcy"), and besides: what good are democratic elections if they're regularly rigged by the office-holders—for crying out loud, they even include the names of the recently deceased in the voters' registry in order to get more votes, and are referred to as royalty when visiting Atlantic City! ("Anastasia")

Nucky may hold a public office that depends on the outcome of an election, but he presides over the Boardwalk like a king, as is stressed numerous times. Agent Van Alden (who, incidentally, relocates to Cicero, Illinois, at the end of the second season), points out that Nucky may be "a county treasurer, but he lives like a pharaoh" ("The Ivory Tower"). On another occasion, Eli remarks that it just takes Nucky a wave of his scepter to get what he wants ("Return to Normalcy") and he mocks his brother as "king fucking Neptune" ("Peg of Old"). When Nucky himself humbly assesses that he considers himself "more of an overseer" whose sole interest is to provide "continuity of leadership" ("The Emerald City") we may take his actual meaning to be: I am the king of Atlantic City—and the head of the city's body politic.

Focusing on the struggle for power and rivalries within families, the gangster genre has been read as the legitimate heir to Shakespearean tragedy. Nucky's comment to his traitorous brother ("Et tu, Eli?") in "To the Lost" is a quote from Shakespeare's play, *Julius Caesar*, but Nucky isn't the only one to honor that tradition. There's the Commodore, with his vision of Atlantic City as "a kingdom on the ocean rising up from the sand" ("Two Boats and a Lifeguard"). There's also Jimmy, who's hailed as "Prince Jimmy" following his near-takeover of power from Nucky. And then there's George Remus, who, like an emperor, refers to himself in the third person.

Not only is Nucky's Atlantic City a haven for men who live like kings and whose temper could make the emperor

Nero look like a choirboy in comparison (or, more accurately, a young fiddle-player), but the town also serves as a model for America at large in the early 1920s: a place afflicted by the Volstead Act, where different political movements clash, where women fight for the right to vote, where organized crime meets organized politics—and where the body politic still appears to be healthy and in good spirits, in spite of germs, venereal diseases, and booze.

10
Absurd Heroes

RACHEL ROBISON-GREENE

War's ugly. It makes us painfully aware of our own suffering and the suffering of other people. Before war occurs, our goals and projects, personal relationships, jobs, habits, and other activities seem to have real value for us. But senseless and needless violence makes us aware that those endeavors ultimately mean very little, if anything at all.

What's real about human experience is that people suffer, and human suffering and even death mean very little in the scheme of things. One moment a person is alive, the next moment they are not. And though we may not be able to forget what we have seen, we must move on with our lives.

Jimmy Darmody, a fictional character in the historically-based HBO series *Boardwalk Empire*, has just returned from World War I at the start of the series. He says of his experience, "It's almost impossible to describe the horror. . . . It's a living, . . . waking . . . nightmare" ("Home"). Just as soldiers do today, Jimmy and the other returning soldiers in the series struggle to find a place in their old lives after experiencing the horrors of war.

It was in the face of war that existential philosophy became increasingly popular. Thinkers with similar positions, such as Nietzsche, Kierkegaard, and Dostoyevsky were writing before the World Wars, but existentialism truly found a home during and in the wake of these conflicts. Existentialist authors such as Sartre, Camus, and de Beauvoir, challenged the traditional Western philosophical understanding of the essence or function of human beings. A common line of thought in western philosophy up to this point was that the key feature, or essence, of a human being is their capacity for rational thought. We are, essentially, rational creatures.

It's easy to see how that notion might go up in flames in the face of the senseless brutality, war. Defining humans in terms of their rationality is too easy, and it ignores one of the most important facts about us—our capacity to create ourselves. As Sartre famously put it "existence precedes essence." What this means is that we do not come into being as a thing with a certain primary function. Rather, we build ourselves. Our choices play a role in determining who we are. Since we are constantly making choices, no definitive essence of any individual is set until that individual is dead. This kind of view may help to better explain how we should understand, say, the Nazi soldier who executes innocent children. Intuitively, it is off-putting to say of such a person that he is, in his very essence, a rational creature. Rather, he is what he has made himself.

Boardwalk Empire is a series that has as its primary focus self-made men and women. Prohibition allows for the satisfaction of certain opportunistic desires and most of the characters are quick to recognize that fact. There are those on the other side of the fence, like Agent Van Alden, who attempt to hold on to the meaningfulness of the law (at least to the extent that a character like Van Alden can consistently keep a grasp on what that means). In real life, and in *Boardwalk Empire*, the way in which a person goes about making themselves may have a lot to do with the extent to which that person believes they can achieve some fundamental meaning in life. And the extent to which they believe in that kind of meaning may have a lot to do with the kind of senseless suffering to which they have been exposed. If a person's exposure is minimal, then human life may seem to have an inherent value. Upon exposure, that perspective may quickly be turned around. In the Season One episode, "Home," Jimmy shares a war story with Liam, a rival gangster:

> There was a soldier, a German; him and his men tried to attack our position in the Argonne forest. It was night-time. While he was trying to climb through some barbwire, I shot him twice; once in the stomach, once in the neck. He slumped over the barbwire, and no matter what he did to try and wriggle free, it just got worse for him. I left him there, like that, for days, listening to him moaning, crying, "Mutti, mutti, mutti," that's German for "mama"; "mama," that's what he kept saying. The curious thing is that despite the fact that his situation was utterly hopeless, he didn't wanna die. I offered to kill him several times, but he just kept fighting. Like some miracle would befall him, get him out of his predicament. We hold on so desperately to life; some people feel, certainly in that soldier's situation, that being alive is much, much worse.

The soldier in the story struggles to hang on to life, even a life such as it is. Jimmy suggests, however, that life as such is not inherently valuable. There are some things worse than death, and in Jimmy's mind, this kind of degrading, honorless, painful life is one of those things.

Jimmy shares this story not so much to make a philosophical point about whether life itself is fundamentally valuable, but to set Liam up to be shot in the head by Jimmy's sniper buddy Richard Farrow. After all, Liam sliced up the face of Jimmy's pretty prostitute girlfriend which ultimately led to her suicide. But the story does reveal something about Jimmy's psychological makeup. By Season Three, the tapestry of Jimmy's life begins to unravel, and we see the full range of backstory that caused his existential crisis. Exposure to the war has a lot to do with it, but as we learn, his wartime experiences don't tell the whole story. One thing is clear even early on in Season One, and that is that Jimmy isn't messing around with fundamental categories like good or bad or right or wrong. We see the kind of man into which Jimmy is trying to make himself.

A common theme in the writing of Albert Camus is the presence of absurdity in our lives. Absurdity, as he defines it, is a conflict between the desires of an individual and an indifferent universe. There are things that we want out of the world. We want our lives to be significant in the scheme of things. We don't want to die and we don't want our loved ones to dies. We don't want to suffer and, by and large, we don't want other decent people to suffer either. But the universe doesn't care about accommodating these desires. The universe isn't even the kind of thing that can care about accommodating these desires. As creatures capable of reflective thought, we recognize this, and when we do, we can potentially become paralyzed by absurdity. This can happen to us, not just in extreme situations like on the battlefield, but in our daily lives. Camus describes such a realization:

> It happens that the stage sets collapse. Rising, streetcar, four hours in the office or the factory, meal, streetcar, four hours of work, work, meal, sleep, and Monday Tuesday Wednesday Thursday Friday and Saturday according to the same rhythm—the path is easily followed most of the time. But one day the "why" arises and everything begins in that weariness tinged with amazement. Weariness comes at the end of the acts of a mechanical life, but at the same time it inaugurates the impulse of consciousness. It awakens consciousness and provokes what follows. What follows is the gradual return to the chain or it is the definitive awakening. At the end of awakening comes, in time, the consequence, suicide or recovery. (*The Myth of Sisyphus*)

Camus points out that there are two very different responses that we can have to the recognition that our existence is absurd. The first response is escapism. We can escape in many ways. One way is to commit suicide, as Richard Harrow almost does. Camus describes the second way to escape absurdity, "The typical act of eluding . . . is hope. Hope of another life one must "deserve" or trickery of those who live not for life itself but for some great idea that will transcend it, define it, give it a meaning, and betray it." Let's see how this approach applies to Agent Van Alden.

The Escapism of Nelson Van Alden

It somehow seems strange to say that Agent Van Alden is deeply religious. After all, he murdered Sebso, his partner at the Bureau of Prohibition. He lusts after plenty of women other than his wife. He stole a hair ribbon from Margaret Schroeder, obviously because of the deep sense of attraction he felt for her. He even got Lucy Danzinger, loose woman and former love interest of Nucky Thompson, pregnant with his child. These certainly don't seem like the actions of a devout conservative Christian—a Christian consumed with snuffing out the flames of sin brought about by the consumption of alcohol.

When the motivations for these actions are fully explained, however, Van Alden's intense commitment to Christianity (albeit a very idiosyncratic view of Christianity) is clear. Sebso's death was no run-of-the-mill drowning. While looking for a distillery, Sebso and Van Alden encounter a group of Christians performing baptisms in the woods. Van Alden comments on Sebso's shoes, hinting at his suspicions. Sebso says he will do anything to prove he is not on the take. Van Alden performs a baptism on Sebso, dunking him over and over, finally dunking him under for so long that he kills him. When he realizes his partner is dead, Van Alden yells, *"THOU HAST FULLFILLED, THE JUDGMENT OF THE WICKED!* ("Paris Green"). I'd say that in this scene he demonstrates some serious religious fervor.

He doesn't let his Season One obsession with Margaret Schroeder get in the way of his religious devotion either. He steals the ribbon from her. He looks at her picture. But he makes sure that he is flogging himself with a belt while he is doing it.

Finally, though it's true that he got Lucy pregnant, he's able to justify the whole thing to himself because his wife, Rose Van Alden is incapable of having children. This is just

God's way of fixing that problem for him. He locks Lucy up in the apartment he keeps in Atlantic City. He doesn't allow her to leave or to pursue any of her own interests at all. When she tells him that she would like to appear in a play (her aspiration is to become an actress) he refuses, saying, "Well, that can't be, because you are carrying a child which is a sacred charge from the Lord and an economic agreement between us." He asserts a kind of moral authority over Lucy in light of his religion, even though he was the one who got her pregnant and is keeping her a prisoner in his apartment.

Embracing the religious life is, for Camus, a form of escapism. To be a Christian is to believe that, though fundamental meaning is not apparent in this life, God exists to imbue life with some special meaning. It may seem that the universe is indifferent to our desires, but, if we live our lives in a particular way, our desires are satisfied in some future life to come.

During prohibition, there was no better place for a person to get their less fundamental desires satisfied than in Atlantic City. When Van Alden's devout wife comes to visit her husband, she's given a pamphlet with the title, "If Jesus came to Atlantic City." The naive couple assumes that it contains a list of all of the religious houses in the city. Instead, it is a listing of all of the whore houses. Of course, both of them are appalled; but enough of Van Alden's characteristics have been revealed at this point for us to know what his desires really are. This is where Van Alden fails the authenticity test. He may be able to deny the absurdity of his existence with his appeal to religion, but in the process, he also must deny important aspects of his character. He must not only deny them, but he must actively fight against them both internally and externally. To do so is to be inauthentic.

Authentic Gangsters

Camus has a second way of dealing with absurdity, and I think that some of the characters in the series, particularly the former soldiers, at least attempt this second kind of response. Before we talk about that, I want to talk about some sort of unique existential problems that return soldiers like Richard and Jimmy face as soldiers, considerations that make it difficult for them to live authentic lives when they come home.

To be inauthentic is to fall into what Sartre calls "bad faith." There are a number of different ways we can fall into bad faith. First, we can define ourselves too much in terms of our facticity. Our facticity consists in the set of facts that are true about us. For example, facts about your past, such as the fact that you were born at a particular time or that you have the biological parents that you have. Much as Jimmy might hate it, the Commodore is his father and Gillian is his mother. A person can be inauthentic, or fall into bad faith with regard to their facticity if they either define themselves to much in terms of their facticity or if they ignore their facticity too much. If Jimmy defines himself too much in terms of the facts of his origin, namely, the Commodore, he might think that he can't live any life other than a life consumed with trying to rule Atlantic City. But if a person ignores their facticity, they ignore parts of themselves that govern the set of real possibilities for them. Lucky Luciano was an employee of Rothstein. If he denies that element of his facticity, he could end up in a world of hurt

We can also fall into bad faith by taking the wrong attitude with regard to our transcendence. Our transcendence is that which we might become. It is by recognizing the transcendence of other individuals that we can understand their actions. For example, I can understand the actions of a student by recognizing their potential for transcendence into a professional. We can fall into bad faith with regard to our transcendence in one of two ways. First, we could fail to recognize our transcendence by defining ourselves too much in terms of our facticity.

Sartre gives an example of a Nazi soldier. The soldier shoots innocent children because he views it as his job. He sees himself as a Nazi soldier. But, in this case, the Nazi soldier fails to recognize something more about himself. He is not just his brute facticity, he is also his transcendence. He has the opportunity to create himself and become something more than a soldier willing to follow any order whatsoever. People can also fall into bad faith by defining themselves too much in terms of their transcendence.

In Sartre's Play *No Exit,* his characters provide models of the various ways that we can fall into bad faith. Three people, Estelle, Ines, and Garcin, are each, individually, escorted into the same room. They learn that this is hell—to occupy the space together for eternity. In life, Garcin was a journalist and saw himself as the type who would put his life on the line to expose the truth. In fact, however, Garcin never did anything brave in his life. He spends his time in the play trying to get the other characters to agree with him that he was a courageous man, but none of them will do it. Garcin denies his facticity (his actual actions in life) in favor of the transcendence that he never achieved. Garcin is in bad faith.

Sartre, among others, points out that we are social beings who can't help but to see ourselves, in part, through the eyes of others. This is both a blessing and a curse. On the one hand, we can be kept honest by recognizing the way that other people see us. Consider an example that Sartre gives. The object of your affection is undressing on the other side of the door. You peek through the keyhole to watch. Then someone comes around the corner and sees you. Their look changes the way you see yourself. You might now see that you were being a pervert or behaving disrespectfully. Hopefully, your actions change as a result of being seen by another person in this case. The look of others can be good for us. On the other hand, it can also propel us into bad faith. If we define ourselves too much in terms of what other people think of us, we fail to recognize that we can be something more.

These forms of bad faith are interrelated. It is easy to shift from one form of bad faith into another. The risk of falling into bad faith may be particularly severe for returning soldiers who have seen and done things that (we would think), those people waiting for them at home did not have to witness. It must be hard, then, to identify with these horrific experiences just enough, but not to let them consume you. A soldier would fall into bad faith if they didn't recognize the horrors they had to experience, but would equally be in bad faith if they failed to see that they could have a full, satisfying life even with those horrors in their memory.

Viewers are exposed to many returned soldiers in *Boardwalk Empire* who are struggling to find this balance. In the Season Two episode "Gimcrack & Bunkum," Jimmy gives a Memorial Day speech to a crowd of citizens, many of them soldiers who are missing limbs. Jimmy says that when people ask him what he did out there, he answers, "I made it back." He proceeds to list the names of soldiers who were not so lucky. As he reads the names, the scene cuts to Richard Harrow, who is looking through the scrapbook he keeps of memories and aspirations. The book is filled with pictures cut out of magazines of families, husbands, wives, and children—an idyllic life that he wants but believes he will never have. The book ends with two pictures, on the left is a painting that Jimmy's wife created of Richard's post-war face without his mask, most of one side missing. On the right is a photograph of Richard the way he looked before he left—strikingly handsome and happy. We are led to wonder if Richard's name should be on the list that Jimmy is reading. He left for war and never really came back—not authentically. Perhaps Jimmy never authentically returned either. Richard and Jimmy are both trapped in bad faith. They're trapped by conceptions of them that other people have—people who do not know war. Richard is trapped by the way people see his face. None of them know the man he was. His community forces him into bad faith, poignantly demonstrating the point that Sartre makes so powerfully at the end of *No Exit* when Garcin exclaims that "Hell is other people."

War Heroes and Absurd Heroes

Camus says, "there is only one real philosophical question, and that is suicide." The challenge is to see whether we can recognize the absurdity of our existence and go on to live authentic lives—lives as free from bad faith as possible—that are subjectively worth living. We have seen one type of response in the escapist strategy of Agent Van Alden. Richard Harrow almost engages in an escapist strategy himself in Season Two when he goes into the woods to kill himself.

There's an alternative to escapism and that's to become an absurd hero. An absurd hero is one who, in full recognition of the absurdity of their situation, chooses to make his response to absurdity his own. The standard example of the absurd hero appears in Camus's "Myth of Sisyphus." Sisyphus is doomed by the Gods to push a boulder up a hill only to watch it roll back down and he must repeat this task over and over again for eternity. Sisyphus responds to the situation by recognizing that his task is absurd, but responding to such a recognition by making his reaction his own and taking each success as a victory. This may be Camus's most famous example of an absurd hero, but closer to what we see in *Boardwalk Empire* is Meursault—the main character from Camus's novel *The Stranger*.

The Stranger begins with the death of Meursault's mother. Mersault is strangely ambivalent to this occurrence, focusing at the funeral on the heat and the length of time that each attendee is present. Other spectators find his behavior strange. Later in the story, he befriends a violent man, a man who kills his girlfriend. Meursault remains friends with the man and when the brother of the murdered woman confronts them, Meursault ends up stabbing him. All the while, Meursault maintains a strange apathetic attitude toward events.

In the final pages of the story, Meursault comes to understand his own strange nature, motivated by a recognition of the nature of the world. He says:

> I looked up at the mass of signs and stars in the night sky and laid myself open for the first time to the benign indifference of the world.

Meursault is sentenced to death and, reflecting on his life, he says, "I had been right I was still right I was always right. I had lived my life one way and I could just as well have lived it another. I had done this and I hadn't done that. I hadn't done this thing and I had done another. And so?" This highlights a distinctive aspect of the absurd hero. Because they recognize that life and the particular endeavors within life have no fundamental meaning, they recognize that one way of living one's life is should not be privileged over any other way. Absurdity conveys equivalence on different lifestyle choices.

Another distinctive feature of an absurd hero is that, because they recognize that there is no fundamental meaning in life, they pursue an ethic of quantity rather than an ethic of quality. Instead of pursuing meaningful things, the absurd hero finds what they like and try to maximize it.

When Jimmy returns from the war, he seeks to become a self-made man. Early on, he tires of being simply Nucky's driver. He wants some real power. In "Paris Green," he derides his father, The Commodore, for never being around when he was growing up. He claims that his father has never really known him. The Commodore replies, "I know you backwards and forwards. You want everything you can get your hands on."

Jimmy's actions are consistent with the Commodore's assessment and are consistent, at least on the surface, with the actions of an absurd hero. He has rejected the idea that specific relationships in his life are supposed to play any sort of real, solid, unwavering role. Gillian is mother or lover. Nucky is father or arch nemesis. Angela is wife and mother of his child, but it is a marriage of convenience and has no more meaning than that. Jimmy's ability to roll with the punches when it comes to his relationships is reminiscent of the sentiment that Meursault expresses in *The Stranger*:

> I often thought that if I had had to live in the trunk of a dead tree, with nothing to do but look up at the sky flowing overhead, little by little I would have gotten used to it.

As a result, Jimmy is able to practice an ethic of quantity, to set out to get the biggest piece of the pie that he can. After returning from the war, the methods involved in Atlantic City politics are familiar if not tame. Jimmy's capable of violence right out of the gate when he arranges for the shipment of alcohol to be hijacked and assists Al Capone in gunning down the people transporting it. Jimmy gets more and more successful as his storyline develops in Season Two.

Richard seems to have motivations similar to Jimmy's. He's willing to kill as needed, his sniper skills come in handy that way. The two seem to have done well in meeting each other, as many other soldiers may not have returned from the war so ruthless.

But are Richard and Jimmy really absurd heroes? Have they really rejected fundamental meaning in order to pursue an ethic of quantity? I think not in the case of Richard, and not until the bitter end in Jimmy's case. They aren't as tough as they want to come across. There is evidence throughout the series that Jimmy is hurt by being let down by just about every person close to him. His relationship with his own son suggests that he thinks that fathers should play real, nurturing roles in the lives of their children.

The Commodore let Jimmy down in every conceivable way, up to and including conceiving him through an act of rape. Nucky let him down by serving as father figure to him and then failing to treat him with any respect in his adult life. His wife didn't even treat him with enough respect to let him know that she was a lesbian. Jimmy has never had a real, secure, nurturing relationship. Perhaps the most tragic and powerful example of what I'm describing here is that disturbing scene in Season Three's "To the Lost," when his mother, someone he should be able to trust above all others, convinces him to have sex with her, insisting to him that "There's nothing wrong with any of it."

This act is essentially a death sentence for Jimmy. He rushes off to war, and, as he suggests later, never really returns. Unlike the absurd hero, Jimmy doesn't, in a cool hour of reflection, accept absurdity and embrace it. Jimmy hasn't resigned himself to anything. He has been systematically destroyed.

Richard Harrow also fails as an absurd hero. Though he certainly seemed to be pursuing an ethic of quantity with Jimmy, in the end, he values meaningful personal relationships perhaps more than any other character on the show. He obsesses over having a wife and children. In the end, his most violent act of all, the mass murder of Gyp Rossetti's entire organization, is an attempt to preserve what he thinks has real value—the life and whatever childlike innocence is left of his best friend's son Tommy.

Like Meursault, however, it seems that in the end, Jimmy really does get it. He really does embrace the absurdity of his existence. At the end of Season Two, Jimmy has lost everything and he is charging toward the cliff's edge on a long hazy, heroin-ridden bender. He kills his father, the Commodore and then passes out. When he wakes up, the body is gone. His mother made it go away. This one last, cathartic act didn't mean anything. Nothing did. He arranges a meet-up with Nucky from which he knows he will never return.

Fittingly, Jimmy meets Nucky at the Atlantic City War Memorial. Like Meursault at the end of the *The Stranger*, Jimmy knows that his death will happen now, and he accepts that calmly. Meursault describes his last interaction with the prison chaplain, "'Have you no hope at all? And do you really live with the thought that when you die, you die, and nothing remains?' 'Yes', I said."

Jimmy too now knows that hope is lost, and indeed, hope never really existed. He calmly advises Nucky on how to deal with his first kill, no longer worrying himself with the fact that his father figure cares about him so little that he is about to shoot him in the head. He brushes aside the significance of Nucky's actions, leaving us with the truth: "I died in the trenches, years back. I thought you knew that."

11
Fighting for Life in Atlantic City

JOHN FITZPATRICK

Early in 1919 Prohibition began in the United States as the Eighteenth Amendment to the Constitution was ratified. This made the sale and distribution of alcohol illegal in the United States. However, since local authorities, particularly in large urban areas, showed little interest in enforcing prohibition Congress in October passed the Volstead act which gave federal authorities the power to arrest the sellers and distributors of alcohol.

But given the lucrative nature of the alcohol trade these federal authorities were ill equipped to counter the efforts of growing criminal enterprises. Prohibition, rightly or wrongly, is often credited with creating the conditions that allowed the tremendous growth in organized crime in the United States. Many of these criminal organizations lasted decades after prohibition was repealed in 1933. Even though *Boardwalk Empire* is historical fiction, it tells this overall story well.

One of the striking features of the universe that *Boardwalk Empire* inhabits is the sheer viciousness and ruthlessness of the Prohibition-era gangsters. This was partly the result of the ineffectiveness of the federal authorities in matching the resources provided by the profits of the alcohol trade. But it's still unclear why human beings who can operate outside the legal system become so vicious and so ruthless. Is this because in absence of civil authority people are naturally this way? What are we like in the absence of governmental regulation and enforcement? What is human temperament like living in a state of nature?

The Modern Era

While the Modern Era of Philosophy, roughly between the years of 1500 and 1900, was a rich era for philosophy in general, it was also a rich period in the development of ethical and political theory. While the theories that were produced in this era can be traced back to the ancient Greeks and Plato, the Modern Era was a period of further refinement. Theorists as diverse as Thomas Hobbes, John Locke, Jean-Jacque Rousseau, Jeremy Bentham, Immanuel Kant, John Stuart Mill, Frederick Engels, and Karl Marx all had important contributions to make.

But one point that can be easily lost is that many of these theorists' disagreements about ethics and politics stem from their different views on what is fundamentally a series of metaphysical questions: does the idea of a fixed and immutable human nature make sense? Or is human nature sufficiently malleable that we can reinvent ourselves to be quite different from what we currently observe? Or is the truth somewhere in the middle?

This is an important issue right at the heart of *Boardwalk Empire*. The Modern era was no stranger to violence and warfare. In fact, one unintended consequence of Martin Luther's launching of the Protestant Reformation by rebelling against the Catholic Church in Germany in 1517 was hundreds of years of warfare between Protestants and Catholics, which continued into the twentieth century with the "troubles" in Ireland. And *Boardwalk Empire* exhibits both aspects in spades.

In the immediate aftermath of World War I we see a tension between the Wasp establishment and the later arriving immigrants of Catholic and Jewish descent. Those that are kept out of the mainstream often seek illegal opportunities for advancement. We see that in the gangs of blacks, Hispanics, and Russians that inhabit our inner cities today. We see it in the Irish, Catholic, German, and Jewish gangs that inhabit our Prohibition-era past. When Jimmy returns from the war, he finds no legitimate path to support his family. Abandoning the opportunity that Princeton might have offered him turns out to be a sucker's move. Our country, now and then, values patriotism as an abstract ideal, but does little for our damaged veterans. The offer of Wal-Mart to give honorably discharged veterans a job is apropos; when Nucky offers Jimmy a "Wal-mart job," he rejects this offer in favor of joining Capone in the botched liquor hijacking that becomes a central thread of the first season.

Modern Ethical Theory and Public Policy

Most of the ethical approaches we find in the Modern Era are ethics of right action. The fundamental ethical question is: What is the right thing to do? Thus, ethical theories that follow from this approach are primarily about right conduct and obligation. So, for example, Ethical Egoism is the view that morality requires us to perform those actions that are in our own rational self-interest. It is hard not to underestimate how powerfully this approach weaves itself through the universe of *Boardwalk Empire*. When Nucky is faced with the problem of Jimmy's exposure over the botched hijacking, his solution allows him to egoistically kill many birds with one stone. He frames someone else for the murders and helps his friend Jimmy. But who to frame? Well, Nucky is quite fond of Margaret and has every reason to get her husband out of the way. But he also enjoys the power of being judge, jury and executioner, so he sends his brother off to murder the wife-battering scum. Help Jimmy, remove a romantic rival, and get to feel self-righteous about it. Not a bad day's work.

Another example is Consequentialism, which is the view that morality requires us to perform those actions that will produce the best consequences when the interests of all relevant parties are considered. The Women's Christian Temperance Union and its members are seen engaged in this kind of reasoning. Alcohol is harmful to the men that consume it and completely destructive to the women and children who rely on these men. However, they underestimated the unintended consequences of Prohibition. The costs of Prohibition exceeded the benefits. Thus, this was a piece of poor consequentialist reasoning and eventually prohibition ended. Ultimately we may end our own drug Prohibition when we realize that the costs exceed the benefits.

A third view of right action, Deontology, holds that morality requires us to follow rules of conduct that conform to duty, obligations and rights. When Nucky wishes to get his pet candidate elected mayor, he asks Margaret to give an essentially dishonest speech to a group of women voters. Eventually she reluctantly agrees to do so, even though she is sure this is wrong. She recognizes that she has in this instance a clear obligation to tell the truth. This is one important point in a longer story arc where Margaret goes from being a person who prides herself on doing the right thing, to becoming one who acts out of primarily egoistic motives.

Social Contract Theory maintains that morality requires us to follow rules of conduct that rational, self-interested people would agree are fair and mutually beneficial. I will agree not to do harmful or unfair things to you if you will make the same agreement with me. There are many examples of this in *Boardwalk Empire*. Season One ends with a truce between Nucky and his enemies. The war has become too expensive, and given their complementary resources it makes more sense to work together. Social contact theory seems to be a particularly rich theory to use in the examination of the universe of *Boardwalk Empire*. When criminals flourish, and there's little respect for the law, it seems almost natural to question whether the existing social contract is meeting the needs of the citizens, and whether a different social contact could better meet those needs. At first glance, it seems that the disrespect for the law that stems from Prohibition undermines the other elements of the social contract that are functional.

In all these cases we're justifying moral conduct through the process of evaluating the morality of their actions. Thus, we can morally evaluate people based on their performing or avoiding those actions that the theory either requires or forbids.

Nasty, Brutish, and Short

Thomas Hobbes in his famous book *Leviathan* asks what humans are like in the absence of any organized government. He concludes that life in this hypothetical 'state of nature' would be a war of every individual against every other individual, and that human existence would be "solitary, poor, nasty, brutish and short."

Hobbes believes this because of four central human features:

1. We have essentially the same needs and wants. You may not like apples or broccoli, but if you are starving you will be glad to have apples and broccoli to eat. You might not like the idea of sleeping in a cave, but sleeping in a dry and windless cave beats sleeping in a field in the middle of a thunderstorm.

2. Many of our needs and wants are for things that are scarce. Some economists have actually used this idea as the foundational point of their discipline. One way of defining economics is "the study of the allocation of scarce resources." Although water is necessary for sustaining human existence and diamonds are not, in a society like ours where water is plentiful and diamonds are rare, water is cheap and diamonds are expensive.

3. We are as individuals of roughly equal power. Our movies and TV shows are full of martial artists who are able to vanquish a mob when the mob attacks the hero two at a time. But if the mob attacks fifty at a time, say, each mob member throwing a stone, there is no fancy move to block fifty attacks at once.

4. We as a species have limited empathy and altruistic tendencies towards others. This final one is controversial but Hobbes believes that it follows from the other points. In the precarious state of nature where violent death is threatened at almost any moment, we are forced to be concerned about our own mortality. Those who are not looking out for number one will not survive.

So the state of nature is a horrid place where violent death seems imminent. We can escape the state of nature only by voluntarily entering into agreements of non-aggression with each other. I will agree not to steal your food, if you will agree not to steal mine. I will agree not to kill your children, if you will agree not to kill mine. But these agreements are worthless unless there is a sovereign power to enforce them. It is only under a social contract enforced by a mighty Leviathan, a powerful state, that humans can find any peace or security. And much of *Boardwalk Empire* plays according to this Hobbesian analysis. If only Dick Cheney were there to give Nucky and the other terrorists their due.

What *Boardwalk Empire* lacks is a powerful Leviathan; even without his personal difficulties, Agent Van Alden would be no match for Nucky. He simply lacks sufficient resources to enforce the central government's laws. Atlantic City is run as Nucky's private fiefdom, and the politicians in Trenton and Washington are largely on his payroll.

Other social contract theorists such as John Locke and Jean-Jacques Rousseau have different views of the state of nature, and would offer a different analysis of the social disintegration during the prohibition era. Locke is less pessimistic than Hobbes about the state of nature. Locke believes that in the state of nature there is little to fight over. Our possessions are limited to what we can carry on our backs. The strong may eat first, but in the absence of modern preservatives there will always be enough to go around. There is no rational motive to hoard.

It's only in a more advanced society that Hobbesian ruthlessness would come into play. In a more advanced society, particularly one with money, it is necessary to develop property rights. So Locke suggests we need, in more advanced cultures, to have a system that ensures property rights by providing a justification for property rights, and then a system for defending them. So the sole legitimate function of government is to establish title to property and negotiate resolutions to disputes about property rights. It is not part of government's responsibility to decide how free people should use their own property as long as they are not infringing on the property rights of others.

Locke argues that when government tries to do more than offer a night watchman state it goes beyond its limited abilities and causes social chaos as free people choose to rebel. Thus, as Locke would see it the chaos that streams through *Boardwalk Empire* is a direct result of the illegitimacy of Prohibition; this paternalistic—the government knows what's best for you—legislation breaks the fragility of the social contract.

Disrespect for property rights is a central feature of Nucky's regime. Legitimate businesses must pay Nucky protection money in order to operate. And when the D'alessio brothers rip off Nucky's bagman it hardly seems criminal. After all, Nucky has no legitimate claim to the cash. This point receives further emphasis when Margaret intervenes on the behalf of Madame Jeunet. Since this "tax" has no legitimate purpose, there is no further injustice in its being applied arbitrarily.

Jean-Jacque Rousseau in his *Discourse on the Origin of Equality* draws a radical contrast between what he calls "savage man" and what he calls "civil man." He believes that in the state of nature humans are "Noble Savages" and that what plays out in *Boardwalk Empire* is a perfect example of how commercial society produces the corruption inherent in "civil man." In the state of nature humans must be strong and resourceful in order to survive. They are indifferent to luxuries and only care about what allows them to live simply and freely. The noble savage has no desires beyond physical needs. Humans in the state of nature have motivations and instincts that are directly tied to nature and guided by an internal understanding of how best to care for themselves. As noble savages we are at peace with nature and at peace with ourselves.

One aspect of Rousseau's philosophy that resonates through *Boardwalk* is the innocence of children and the complete corruption of adult society. Children enter the world as noble savages, and are brought into the lies and machinations of the adults. Nucky's decision to burn down his father's house seems apropos. Of course, Margaret's innocent son must be exposed to this plot.

The innocence of noble children can be contrasted with the "civilized" adults. We civilized adults are always agitated and anxious and constantly tormented. We work ourselves into an early grave because we're so concerned about "power and reputation." Rousseau looks at his society and sees emotional turmoil and a general disregard for our own wellbeing. The excessive labor of the poor, the dangerous softness of the rich, foul and polluted cities with their epidemic diseases, and tainted food are examples Rousseau uses to show the corrupting nature of city life.

It seems that while the noble savage is amoral but basically good, civilized humans are immoral and clearly evil. The noble savage lacks vices and virtues except for the sole natural virtue of pity. This lack of sophistication when softened with pity leaves humans in the state of nature at home with nature and our companions. But civilized humans in commercial society find themselves constantly in competition with each other. The wealthy man whose children look forward to his death, the merchant who profits when disasters befall competitors, and people who enjoy the misery of their neighbors are all examples given by Rousseau of how civilization produces inhuman desires. Every war, disease, and natural disaster will prove profitable to some at the expense of others and thus be relished by the profiteers. Rousseau agrees with Locke that the problem arises with private property, but does not see how the free market can produce neutral arbiters. It is always profitable for someone to game the system.

This bleak picture of civilized humans is fully consistent with the moral universe of *Boardwalk Empire*. Why does the Klan attack Chalky White? Primarily because they enjoy the suffering of black people. It pleases their egos to see others as inferior. We can also see that invariably one gangster profits from the misfortunes of others. Early on in *Boardwalk Empire* we see the value to Nucky of having his brother in control of local law enforcement. He can have other bootleggers and smugglers arrested, and thus increase his own profits. He can use this law enforcement connection to protect his allies like Chalky. And law enforcement can be used to help Chalky seek revenge on the clan.

So we see that these conflicting views of the state of nature can be found in *Boardwalk Empire*. Hobbes's vision is well represented in the gangland violence and the continued war of all against all that is the result of no powerful central governing authority. Rousseau's vision is well represented in the corrupt nature of commercial society. And Locke's vision is well represented in the chaos of a society unable to protect the property rights of its citizens.

But two later theorists thought that the state of nature has nothing to do with the political problems of commercial society. Karl Marx believed that the "superstructures of social organization" are based on the "means of production" currently available. And John Stuart Mill believed that with the proper education and upbringing we can potentially be much more than the "starved specimens' we currently are. It's largely irrelevant what we were like prior to civil society. Both of these thinkers believed that human beings are highly malleable, and are largely shaped by their environments. Human beings are not naturally this or that, but even if we were, we would be something else in a different social structure. And this may be the most vivid theme of *Boardwalk Empire*. What Margaret was like naturally seems irrelevant to what she becomes later on, after Nucky's influence and corruption.

But the great transformation from Season One to the end of Season Two is the transformation of Nucky himself. Early in Season One Jimmy tells Nucky that it's no longer possible to be half a gangster. By the time he assassinates Jimmy at the end of Season Two he has become a gangster and a half. Nucky begins the series as a corrupt politician, but perhaps ultimately a force for the good. He seems to care about his city, and about the welfare of its citizens. But Prohibition and subsequent events have changed him. And if this is the story that *Boardwalk Empire* tells, then what Nucky and other humans *would* have been like in the state of nature is largely irrelevant.

Part IV

From Our Cellars

12
The Women of *Boardwalk Empire*

RACHEL ROBISON-GREENE

Boardwalk Empire is dominated by male characters. The main gangsters are men and so are their cronies. The female characters have important story arcs, but most of the time those plot lines matter because of the consequences that they bring about for the male characters.

In many ways this fact is unsurprising. The show is about a time in history at which women were struggling to have their voices heard, most notably in the form of the vote. On the other hand, in many ways the historical conditions that make the story being told in *Boardwalk Empire* even possible—namely, Prohibition—was brought about, in no small part, by the voice of women and their opposition to the consumption of alcohol.

Simone de Beauvoir in the *The Ethics of Ambiguity* and *The Second Sex,* challenges the traditional patriarchal social system. She emphasizes the need for women to take an active role in their own liberation. The women of *Boardwalk Empire* are, for the most part, terrible at this. At a time when women were coming together to end oppression, the main female characters of *Boardwalk* are remarkably adept at contributing to that oppression.

Beauvoir on the Boardwalk

Beauvoir's insights regarding the plight of women might be of use to characters like Lucy, Gillian, and Margaret. It would be important for them, from the outset, to recognize that we are all, at our core, free. To fail to recognize our own freedom is to be in, what Beauvoir and her lifelong partner Jean-Paul Sartre, call "bad faith." (For a closer look at Sartre's notion of bad faith, see Chapter 10 in this book.) We can fall into bad faith in any of a number of ways. We might associate too strongly with facts about ourselves, not recognizing the possibility for change. We might also focus on what we may become, without enough focus on the facts by which we're constrained.

The source of bad faith that Beauvoir is most concerned with, however, is the bad faith that we enter into as a result of our relationships with other people. We are social creatures and the viewpoints of others have an impact on how we see ourselves. We are all born into a world with certain social arrangements that have been pre-established. Such arrangements can be beneficial, but they also carry with them the potential for causing us to fall into bad faith.

Certain powerful players in society have, essentially, written the rules. They have created the power structure that we were born into. They formulate the very parameters of our discourse. This can easily lead to oppression. Powerful figures create the category of "the other." Such powerful figures recognize themselves as essential; they identify themselves as "the One" and define those that are not like them as inessential. Consider the treatment of the African American characters in *Boardwalk*. White individuals with power have turned this population into "the Other," such that their very lives are deemed unimportant, understood as so inessential by the Ku Klux Klan, that their lives aren't even assigned any value.

But we began our discussion of this topic with the recognition that we are, at the core of our being, free. We have the power to change our situation. At first glance, this seems a little harsh. When oppression occurs, should we put blame to any degree on the oppressed? Doesn't this just add insult to injury? If however, the goal really is to end the oppression, the people who have the real power and incentive to stop it are the oppressed themselves. However, social conditions can make the exercise of our freedom very, very difficult. For example, facts about our socioeconomic circumstances can make it difficult for us to exercise our freedom.

What's required is what Beauvoir calls "an appeal." We must be able to call to "the other" and struggle against those who would silence us. As individuals who are free, we must be able to connect to each other *as* free individuals. When I, from the position of freedom call upon your free self and demand justice, I change your situation. You may reject my appeal, but you can't change the fact that I have appealed. The success of our projects is determined by the extent to which those projects are adopted and pursued by others. When the appealing voices are loud enough, oppression can be brought to an end. Appeals, however, can only occur between equals, so if we want to end oppression, we have to work as hard as we can for conditions of equality.

Beauvoir is careful to point out, however, that equality is not a synonym for sameness. To be independent, women must recognize two things. First, they must recognize that independence doesn't require that women behave like men. Women do not need to take on what are traditionally considered to be "male traits" in order to end their oppression.

Second, women must not be passive in their socialization as women. Men shouldn't get to fix the discussion regarding what it is to be a woman. As Beauvoir says, "One is not born but becomes a woman."[1] Women should play an active role in determining what it means to be a woman. For example, historically, people have claimed that men are the stronger sex. Part of the definition of what it is to be a man, then is to be strong, and part of the definition of what it is to be a

---

[1] *The Second Sex*, Simone de Beauvoir (Random House, 2010).

woman is to be weaker. But, Beauvoir points out, women weren't involved in that discussion.

What is strength? If it has to do with physical stature, then perhaps men are generally stronger because men are generally bigger. But what if strength were measured in terms of longevity? In that case, as women tend to live longer, women might turn out to be stronger. The goal is for groups that are traditionally oppressed to try to bring about conditions of equality so they can involve themselves in those kinds of conversations.

The particular way in which women's freedom is situated makes it very difficult to avoid oppression. A special relationship in this case exists between 'the one" and "the other" in this particular form of oppression that doesn't exist in the case of "the one" and different types of "others." Women and men are (in many cases) sexually attracted to one another. They fall in love with one another. They produce children and raise those children with one another. It may be particularly difficult to appeal for oppression's end when the person doing the oppressing is your life partner.

Women need to come together, to appeal in solidarity for equality. A further obstacle stands in the way, however, and that obstacle is happiness. Many women are happy in their other-ness. Many women embrace the sense of womanhood that they were given, that they were born into. de Beauvoir says, "Thus woman may fail to lay claim to the status of subject because she lacks definite resources, because she feels the necessary bond that ties her to man regardless of reciprocity, and because she is often very well pleased with her role as the Other."

This is a problem that plagues the main female characters of *Boardwalk Empire*. Let's look at the extent to which these ladies contribute to their own oppression.

Lucy on the Boardwalk with Diamonds

One problem that we can identify from the outset for the ladies of *Boardwalk Empire* is that they are remarkably isolated. Many of them are, in their day-to-day lives, confined to their homes to care for their children. However there is no one who is more isolated than Lucy Danziger when she is basically put under house arrest by Agent Van Alden. The kind of solidarity Beauvoir advocates between women isn't easy to achieve when one isn't even permitted to see other people.

But that isn't even where her story begins. At the beginning of the series, we're introduced to Lucy in her role as Nucky's lover. Lucy is a showgirl who is attractive, but whiny and not very bright. She enjoys the glamorous life that she has with Nucky. She gets fancy dresses and lingerie at *Belle Femme*, Madame Jeunet's dress shop that later plays a prominent role in Margaret's character development. Nucky provides her with material goods, and in exchange, Lucy keeps the bedroom hot. There is no real indication that Nucky feels anything resembling love for Lucy. In fact, in the early episodes of Season One, it's very clear that he's developing feelings for another woman, Margaret Schroeder. Nucky is a widower who wanted to have a child. In "Broadway Limited," perhaps recognizing that she is losing Nucky's attention, Lucy offers to have a child for him. Nucky doesn't take her up on her offer.

Nucky does not respect Lucy. In "Anastasia," Nucky discusses the topic of women's right to vote with his politician friends. Lucy is not able to discuss the topic with any competence and the men laugh her off, suggesting that she has furthered the case that women wouldn't know what to do with the right to vote.

It is difficult also, to achieve any sort of solidarity with other women if you don't desire in any way to be friends with, or to positively interact with, other women. Lucy appears to view all other women as competitors in a grab for the affections of men. In Season One, Nucky is aware that, because he had Margaret's husband, Hans, murdered, Margaret no longer has any real way to support her family, and to help her out he obtains a job for her at *Belle Femme*. As Lucy tries on lingerie at the shop, she treats Margaret as an inferior, derisively sharing with her that Nucky is "a soft touch with the charity cases" ("Broadway Limited"). Later, in "Family Limitation," Lucy is again shopping at *Belle Femme,* and demands that Margaret model some lingerie for her. She then goes on to make hurtful comments about Margaret's body. Lucy is hardly the kind of woman that would be successful in bringing about what Beauvoir had in mind.

Lucy's relationship with Nucky ends and she begins a relationship with Van Alden. Lucy's exactly the kind of woman that Van Alden has the most disdain for, but is, at the same time, the kind of woman he desires the most. Lucy has sex with Van Alden in exchange for money. She becomes pregnant with his child and the two begin an "economical relationship," by which Van Alden pays her to carry the baby to term.

Men are Lucy's main source of income. Alas, she is one of the women whom Beauvoir describes—women who are so consumed with happiness that they are willing to do away with liberty. Lucy isn't doing women any favors by reinforcing "the one's" ideas of what women should be. The type of woman Lucy should be, according to her male admirers, is loud in the bedroom and quiet everywhere else. Lucy seems happy to oblige, so long as the glamorous lifestyle is maintained.

A Mother's Touch

Gillian Darmody is an interesting case. In many ways, she seems to be able to manipulate the men in her life very well. She uses her sexuality as a source of power. She's able to control otherwise incontrollable men such as the Commodore, Lucky Luciano, and Gyp Rossetti. She is very clever and is skilled at using the very expectations that men have of her against them. For example, she's able to use Gyp Rossetti's masochistic fetish against him, putting him in a submissive position so that she can inject him with a high dose of heroin. She moves too slowly, and she is caught and injected herself, but her ability to manipulate a powder-keg like Rossetti is impressive.

Gillian's ability to change in response to changing situations and pressures is truly remarkable. On the face of it, it seems that Gillian exercises her freedom more than any other female character on the show. We might want to say that she exercises her freedom, even if the ways in which she exercises it make us shudder. She moves from mother to lover (or, perhaps more appropriately, rapist), from seductress to caregiver (in the case of the Commodore), from grandmother to mother (in Tommy's case). From afar, it seems like no one can control Gillian. Gillian is the one in control.

The show gives us more intimate moments, however, where we can see that Gillian is not as together as she appears to be. In "What Does the Bee Do?" she becomes the Commodore's caregiver after he suffers a stroke. It must be a difficult situation to be in, to provide care to the man who raped you when you were just a child. As the Commodore lies in bed, incapacitated, Gillian asks him if he remembers the night he raped her. She describes the event and how terrifying it was for her as a child. She loses control and begins to beat the Commodore repeatedly about the head.

Another moment where Gillian's real psychological state is more obvious is in the finale of Season Three, after Gyp Rossetti turned her own heroin syringe on her. When Nucky finds her, she seems to have regressed to her thirteen-year-old self, as if it's the night she was raped.

Though she appears strong and resourceful, Gillian is perhaps, the female character who suffers from bad faith the most. The Commodore changed the facts of her life forever, and in many ways, the fact of her rape consumed her. She never considered that she could be some other, better person. Instead, though she's able to change in changing circumstances, she remains in each case exactly what men want her to be, an object for sexual desire and gratification. She is so trapped in this role that she can't even recognize that it doesn't apply to her own son. She has so many admirers, so many people who think she is the best in the world at playing the role that she plays, yet, she confesses to Jimmy right before she has sex with him that she is "just the loneliest person on earth."

I Ain't Gonna Work on Maggie's Farm No More

The female character with the most potential to help bring about the kind of change that Beauvoir has in mind is Margaret Schroeder. She's smart and resourceful and she understands the nature of oppression. Nucky came to her attention when he came to speak to the Temperance League, of which she was a member. Margaret knew first-hand the problems that could be caused by alcohol. Her husband was an alcoholic who hit her when he was drunk. The Temperance League was, in many ways, very successful. Margaret knows the power of coming together in solidarity and of making the kind of appeal for justice that Beauvoir talks about.

Moreover, Margaret is well spoken and well read. Lucy botches her attempts to justify women's right to vote in "Anastasia," but in that same episode, Margaret is able to speak on the topic with eloquence, impressing Nucky's friends.

She also has a strong desire for justice, though Nucky is able to gradually corrupt her. Nucky's world takes her by surprise at first. Early on, she realizes that the Nucky who gave the speech at the Temperance League is not the real Nucky. Bit by bit, she learns that he is involved in smuggling and selling alcohol. Nucky is kind to her and helps to ensure that she's taken care of financially. She gets increasing swept into his world until she becomes his mistress, and eventually his wife. Once this happens, she's entirely financially dependent on him.

Like Lucy, Margaret is attracted to the glamorous lifestyle. But, as Beauvoir notes, sometimes when women seek happiness in their relationships with men, they give up liberty. We watch Margaret struggle with this repeatedly in the series. She seems on the verge of leaving Nucky at various points, and she keeps a nest egg of money throughout most of their relationship, suggesting that she might really leave if she managed to build up the courage. She has every intention of taking the kids and running away with Owen before his head is mailed to Nucky in a cardboard box.

In Season Two, the couple seems to be reasonably happy. From all appearances, Nucky is motivated strongly to be a good partner for Margaret and a father to their children. What we learn at the end of the season, however, is that Nucky really needs to marry Margaret for legal reasons. We see Nucky is no warm-hearted family man when he is willing to kill Jimmy, who he cared for as a son throughout childhood. Deception aside, however, Margaret appears happy with this new, warmer Nucky. Here again, it is easy to countenance oppression when we're happy in it.

Though Lucy and Gillian may be beyond saving, there is hope for Margaret. In Season Three, we see her actively taking steps to protect women's reproductive rights and to promote education regarding reproductive safety. We see her make an appeal, speaking out on the issue to doctors (much to Nucky's consternation) and to other women in the form of classes at the hospital.

Perhaps even more importantly, at the end of Season Three, Margaret leaves Nucky. Unlike Lucy and Gillian, she now recognizes that, if she continues to be financially dependent on Nucky, she remains in bad faith (though she, of course, would not use this language.) While he continues to dictate the terms of their relationship and to define what her role as a woman is in that relationship, she will never be truly free.

Nucky seems to genuinely care about her, and in the finale of Season Three, "The Best You Could Do Is Not Lose," he comes to her one bedroom apartment where she is staying with her children. He offers her a wad of cash telling her to take it, insisting that it doesn't mean anything. "Yes it does," she insists, and shuts the door in his face. Simone de Beauvoir would be proud.

13
Gillian's Changes

CHELSI BARNARD ARCHIBALD

I didn't spend my life getting groped by a bunch of drunks to wind up in a goddamn poorhouse.

—GILLIAN DARMODY

Boardwalk Empire is largely a man's world. However, women like Margaret Schroeder, Angela Darmody, Lucy Danziger, and Gillian Darmody each possess unique survival skills within the confines of that world. Most of these women carefully toe the line, only occasionally stepping beyond societal expectation. Gillian Darmody is the exception.

Due to the trauma of her youth, a rape at age thirteen, and a subsequent pregnancy as well as her lifelong connections to major players in the underground world, Gillian holds a sense of power that most women would find impossible. One could say that she is a woman playing a man's game.

In Plato's *Phaedo*, he suggests that things are only destroyed by being dismantled into their constituent parts and although the soul is immortal, the body can go through cyclical change in order to adapt and survive. Birth and death are merely binary opposites within this cycle, but have no effect on the soul. For Gillian, her mental denial of traumatic events and her ability to compartmentalize the dismantling of her psyche allow her a survival sense that continually gives way to new mutations of form and function. She sees Jimmy as both a son and a lover, because her ongoing adaption and metamorphosis allow her to shift in between roles, avoiding typical feminine emotional attachment or moral culpability.

Gillian can calculate the unthinkable, making her one of the most dangerous and unpredictable players in a game against her male counterparts. Her ability to stay mentally ahead of men like the Commodore, Nucky Thompson, Lucky Luciano, and Gyp Rosetti shows that for Gillian, every ending represents a new beginning, a new opportunity to shift into another role and begin the dance again.

In the episode "What Does the Bee Do?," Gillian Darmody performs a dance in front of the Commodore, the man who raped her as a thirteen-year-old child and then impregnated her. Gillian's life was inextricably changed forever due to this incident. Gillian dances provocatively for the old man, asking him why he never came to see her perform. She then follows that question with a statement, "I understand. I always have."

She warns the Commodore by telling him the mythos of the virginal Diana, who turned her oppressor into a stag and allowed his own hounds to tear him to pieces. As powerful and intelligent as the Commodore is in business matters he is distracted by Gillian's sexual prowess and misses her warning. Gillian uses this dance to entrance him, to entrap him, and to convince him to do her bidding. Before the man starts having a stroke from his arousal, she demands that he take care of her son. Gillian uses this particular dance as a means to control, but she uses a continual metamorphosis throughout life to shift in and out of differing roles in order to survive.

Plato's *Phaedo*

In Plato's famous dialogue *Phaedo*, he recounts the story of Socrates's death and details the nature of the afterlife as well as arguing for the soul's immortality. He notes that Forms that are abstract, like the soul, are invariable and incomposite and can never be truly dismantled. Only variable objects like the body can be dismantled into constituent parts. Although the soul is immortal, the body can go through a series of cyclical changes in order to adapt and survive. Birth and death are merely binary opposites within this cycle, but have no effect on the soul.

Gillian Darmody is a great representation of this process described by Plato, in that her actions come through a series of births and deaths, leaving her the opportunity to adapt and change. The most significant aspect of Gillian's character is the event of her rape at age thirteen. In "What Would the Bee Do?" Gillian's dance consists of a power struggle between her and the Commodore wherein her only weapon of control is her sexuality. The irony of this is that her path was set on sexual survival due to the Commodore's abuse toward her when she was a child. However, after the Commodore suffers a stroke, the power structure changes and Gillian immediately realizes that the old man now must rely upon her physically in order to survive and she shifts into a new role of caretaker.

When power players Jimmy and Eli worry about placating the Commodore's associates, she orders the men to calm down and she refuses to have the old man taken to a hospital, already assuming a newfound power position. She then insists upon caring for him and assures the worried men that business will be run as usual. Now she's left alone with the Commodore and begins for the first time in over twenty years to speak with him about the night she was raped.

She recounts the way he seduced her as a child, emphasizing that she was dreaming of the waves in a childlike manner and that he wooed her into bed with wine. Prior to her rape, it is assumed that Gillian was merely a child and a pageant girl who didn't know of or need men in order to survive. At this point she is acknowledging a prior shift in her life, from child to adult. She goes on to describe that after the Commodore pinned her down and silenced her screams he raped her. "Do you remember that night?" Gillian asks. The Commodore is clearly incapacitated and not at his full mental clarity, stricken with fear when he realizes Gillian's sudden anger. Whether or not he comprehends what she is asking or remembers the night in question, Gillian begins to slap him into submission while reveling in her small yet newfound sense of control. The incident of rape is Gillian's first form of death in a series of deaths and rebirths, which allows her to mutate into several forms and functions.

Argument of Opposites

Plato recounts that things continually go from living to dead and *vice versa*. The living things must go from being dead to being living through a process of coming to life. In order to live again, we must die or new life is impossible. Nothing is created or destroyed with birth or death, but rather it is broken up into constituent parts and changed within a binary context. Simply put, the changing shape of, say, a body or a circumstance is variable and inconsequential because the soul is immortal, invariable, and can adapt throughout these binary changes of birth and death.

For Gillian, her survival in a man's world is a balance between opposites and is part of a crucial order in the universe. Plato reminds us that the universe is in a state of constant flux. In fact, the only constant in the universe is change. Gillian seems to be innately aware of this and abides by it with the greatest of ease. Her lack of emotional connections to tragic events seems horrific, but it allows her to dance in between roles and shift into new forms. Plato would refer to this as the Theory of Recollection or an inherent knowledge the soul has gathered over a series of lifetimes. She utilizes relationships with Nucky Thompson, Lucky Luciano, and eventually Gyp Rosetti to move up within the social structure of the underground world. In order for Gillian to move into a new realm of power within Atlantic City she must experience some form of change or a rebirth. She experiences several of these instances throughout her lifetime.

Once Gillian is raped she becomes a new person who learns to adapt and survive according to the inherent knowledge that she has gained. Where the child in her dies with the abuse she experiences, a new child named Jimmy is born whom she is meant to care for. It is revealed that Nucky Thompson takes on most of the parenting duties while Gillian earns money and survives by courting other rich and powerful men, a pattern which she adapts to after her experience with the Commodore.

The opposite occurs for Gillian, in that she trades her own childhood to care for her new child, Jimmy. And with the Commodore's stroke she trades her sexual prowess in order to coerce her oppressor into letting her care for him as a weakling whom she now can control without the need to exploit herself. However, Gillian's series of metaphorical deaths and rebirths are more numerous than these two incidents alone. Gillian also uses the Commodore's stroke as an opportunity to put her son Jimmy in a power position over the old man's cronies, essentially giving way to new leadership.

Theory of Forms

Plato's Theory of Forms otherwise known as Theory of Ideas, states that abstract concepts, such as beauty, courage, justice, and goodness exist as immaterial and unchanging ideas. Instances of beauty in the world are only imperfect reflections of the Form of Beauty and are only beautiful insofar as they participate within that Form. The Form of Beauty itself is perfectly and unalterably beautiful, regardless of material changes.

For Gillian, forms can change in objects as much as they can change in people. A specific example is her relationship with Jimmy, whom she tends to treat as an equal in terms of age, responsibility, and friendship rather than a son in need of parenting. For all intents and purposes, Jimmy represents a Form that is interchangeable according to her convenience rather than an actual human being. At one point Gillian reveals to Angela that when Jimmy was a baby she would change his diaper and "kiss his little winkie" ("21"). Angela seems troubled by this, but doesn't question Gillian further.

Viewers may have been disturbed by Gillian's behavior towards her son upon her introduction to the series.

When Jimmy returns from World War I he visits his mother at Café Beaux Arts, where she entertains men with her burlesque troupe. She jumps onto Jimmy in the way a lover would, wrapping her legs around him. Their interactions involve kissing throughout the series in more intense ways than mothers and sons would usually be comfortable with.

The presumption here is that due to Gillian's loss of innocence at such a young age, she has never been able to view Jimmy as a son, but more as a peer and later on as a lover. Where he should be seen as her child he is instead seen as her partner in life, much like a lover or a husband would. The concept of son never seems to fully affect Gillian and she certainly doesn't want to be recognized as a grandmother, which she reminds Angela of early on in the series ("Anastasia").

It isn't until a flashback episode in which Jimmy and Angela have just found out they're pregnant while attending Princeton that viewers understand the full scope of Gillian's blighted outlook ("Under God's Power She Flourishes"). Gillian visits Jimmy at college and after a night of heavy drinking, needs his assistance to get into bed. He worries that she won't remember the evening, but Gillian replies by stating, "I always remember everything, no matter what." Just like her warning to the Commodore during her dance that she has "always known," this is another reference to Gillian's inherent knowledge formed throughout continual deaths and rebirths. Jimmy helps her disrobe and she reminds him "there is no one else in all the world. There's only you and me." As she lies down to sleep she pulls him in, forcing him to kiss her, while repeating to him, "There's nothing wrong with any of it."

Jimmy is so confused by this incident that he immediately enlists in the army and heads off to war, even telling the enlistment officer that both his mother and father are gone and to list Angela as his next of kin. What viewers previously thought was Jimmy's attempt to escape fatherhood actually turns out to be an escape from his incestuous mother. Later on in the same episode, we witness Jimmy's continual downfall as he deals with Angela's murder.

Gillian doesn't acknowledge Angela's death as emotionally damaging or difficult for her son, but rather as an inconvenience, which they will explain to Tommy as his "mother running away to Paris with friends," even suggesting that in a month or two Tommy won't even remember who Angela was. Jimmy strangles his mother in protest repeating, "I'll remember" over and over again before being attacked by the Commodore whom he then kills upon Gillian's request. To Gillian, Angela is merely another Form, which is replaceable and recognizable only as a role that was played in Jimmy's life, the role of wife, lover, or mother to his child. These are all things of which Gillian sees herself fit for in regards to Jimmy. In Gillian's eyes, Angela's death is merely an opportunity for rebirth, to step in and fulfill these roles in order to move ahead with her current agenda.

When Jimmy awakens from a dreamy haze, his wounds have been cleaned and the Commodore's body has been discarded. Tommy and Gillian approach him and the boy asks for his mother. Gillian replies to her grandson saying, "I'm right here" implying that from this point forward, the two will tell Tommy that Gillian is his mother. Jimmy recognizes that his mother is attempting to eliminate Angela's memory, but is so confused, grief-stricken, and influenced by his recent heroin addiction that he does not correct her. While Jimmy tries to grasp the situation Gillian carries Tommy away saying, "One day soon he won't be a little boy anymore. It happens just like that." It is almost as if Tommy is Gillian's young prodigy and Jimmy realizes that he too is replaceable.

While Jimmy obviously exhibits confusion after a life of inappropriate exposures to the world and changing situations, that which he has learned from his father figure, Nucky Thompson, has given him a sense that his mother's behavior is far from normal. Gillian is essentially self-raised, an adaptable animal who shapeshifts and mutates into different forms in order to best suit her immediate needs at any given time. To Gillian, roles serve as Forms rather than permanent assignments and she can interchange them as often as she likes with no emotional attachment or moral culpability. It is a learned survival technique developed at a young age and something that has served her well. While Jimmy finds his mother's dismissal of Angela's death barbaric and cruel, Gillian views death as an imperfect reflection of Form and not the actual permanent loss of a human being.

This is especially discernible with the death of her son Jimmy. When Jimmy leaves his family he must know that he is going to his death as he leaves behind his military-issued dog tags. It's uncertain whether Gillian understands or interprets his leaving as his death. When she is questioned about her estate and the Artemis Club by her accountant she claims that it is in her son's name and that he is away on business. Never is there any indication that Gillian believes Jimmy is actually dead and gone for good. Yet again, Jimmy is a Form that can change shape or purpose according to her current needs. It's more befitting that Gillian see Jimmy as alive and well elsewhere in the universe than dead and gone.

It isn't until it becomes an ongoing issue of Jimmy's whereabouts in regards to the estate that Gillian finally goes into action to replace Jimmy yet again. She meets Roger McAllister, a young man who eerily resembles Jimmy in many ways and she invites him to her home to be her lover. It is interesting to note that when Gillian's power is in question she shifts back into a sexual mode of control in order to achieve her goal. At the moment, she needs her sexuality to seduce Roger so that she can make her final move.

Very little is known about Roger other than he was born in Indiana, traveled from Idaho to Montana to California to Mexico for work and most importantly, he has no familial ties or family that would know of his whereabouts. To Gillian, he is the perfect target for a bait and switch.

Gillian asks Roger if he had a nickname back home and he replies that he did not. She tells him that she will call him 'James' because "he was a king." After inviting Roger over for Easter Sunday and making him dinner, the two make love yet again in the bedroom and he asks about her husband. He is referring to the man who left her such a massive estate, but she answers that the two "knew each other since we were children" and that she was older than the man in question. Gillian obviously is not referring to the Commodore, but is replacing her relationship with Jimmy as filler for the relationship to a so-called husband. She then says that "he walked out one night and I never saw him again."

There are a few things viewers can gather from Gillian's words about her son. She is either delusional and, in an act of psychological survival, truly believes that Jimmy has left and not actually died, or she has convinced herself of the former regardless of what she knows to be true. In Gillian's mind, Jimmy is not her son, a man, or someone who has died. He is rather to her an interchangeable being or Form, which is invariable. He can change appearances, roles, and situations accordingly while still staying uniquely Jimmy. In a sense, Jimmy is not a person to Gillian, but merely a true Form of her ideal which can never be tarnished or damaged, but only changed into what suits her best. Whatever body he encompasses at the moment is insignificant to her because Jimmy always represents the ideal regardless of his appearance. Such is the value of Forms.

Gillian prepares a bath for Roger in the mansion and makes him feel as comfortable as possible before injecting him with a large amount of heroin ("Sunday Best"). She then drowns Roger and places Jimmy's military-issued dog tags around his neck before setting up the scene as a heroin overdose. The body is found by one of Gillian's female employees and Gillian has him cremated at the Coroner's Office. When she asks Richard Harrow if he has any last words for Jimmy he replies, "Jimmy deserved better than this," indicating that he knows this is not Jimmy and that Gillian has performed a bait and switch. Whether or not Gillian believes that this man's body is not the body of her actual son remains to be seen.

Richard Harrow had attempted to be an anchor for Gillian and Tommy since the death of Angela, but was continuously thwarted in his efforts by Gillian. If he were to tell

Tommy about his mother, Gillian would correct Richard and remind Tommy that in fact, she is his rightful mother. It is only after Gillian has banned Richard from the house and is at the mercy of Gyp Rosetti and his dangerous gang that she realizes her mistake. Tommy refuses to come to her or talk to her and she resigns to giving in sexually to Gyp in order to convince him to let her leave with the boy ("Margate Sands").

It is in Gyp Rosetti that Gillian seems to have met her match. His penchant for S&M style sexual escapades may frighten Gillian but she keeps her resolve. In Gyp's moment of weakness she attempts to inject him with heroin like she did with Roger, but this time Gyp is onto her and injects her with the drug instead. What happens following the incident is not only fascinating, but heartbreaking to witness, even for those who have been appalled by Gillian's unquestionably merciless wrath in the past. Nucky and Eli come to the mansion to survey the scene. Richard Harrow has killed nearly every man in the house in order to save Tommy, and Gillian is left amongst the bodies, still inebriated on heroin.

Nucky asks her who is responsible for the scene and Gillian replies, "You came. I was good. I went upstairs like you said to . . . and the man . . . Nucky he did something very bad to me." Thompson is confused by Gillian's reply, but viewers who are aware of her history will recognize that she has reverted back to the evening in her childhood when the Commodore drugged her with wine, sent her upstairs, and then raped her. With Gillian's loss of control of every aspect of her life and the continual deaths and rebirths of form and function she seems to have finally come to an impasse, rare and momentary though it may be.

It can also be argued that Gillian's momentary loss of control is due to her inebriation, something that is rare for her. Unlike the incident with heroin, Gillian's actions at Princeton can be questioned as viewers can't be fully sure that she wasn't using her alleged drunkenness to control Jimmy at the time. This incident is a clear indication of Gillian out of her element. According to the Argument of Opposites and the binary context, if Gillian is currently out of control then she is experiencing yet another death and is not currently alive. There's no question however, that Gillian is a seasoned player in this game and will be reborn with new purpose and begin her infamous dance again.

Part V

Heady Cocktails

14
Two Kinds of Violence in *Boardwalk Empire*

DEBORAH MELLAMPHY

We all have to decide for ourselves how much sin we can live with.

> —NUCKY THOMPSON, "A Return to Normalcy"

One of the first things we learn about Enoch "Nucky" Thompson, played by Steve Buscemi, is that he's a highly duplicitous character.

In the pilot episode, we're introduced to him as he speaks to the Women's Temperance League of Atlantic City about the evils of alcohol and the pursuit of Christian values. The League address him as "Our esteemed Treasurer, the honorable Enoch Thompson" and he recalls a tale from his childhood of the time he had to kill three wharf rats to feed himself, which garners him gasps of sympathy from the crowd.

He appears in this scene as the embodiment of hard work and strict religious beliefs, as well as sobriety, and it's clear that he is very well respected by the group. Yet, when his driver Jimmy Darmody, played by Michael Pitt, calls him away from his speech this image of poverty is quickly debunked when he replies to Jimmy's sympathy with: "First rule of politics kiddo, never let the truth get in the way of a good story."

The pilot episode begins on December 31st, 1919, the day before Prohibition is to take effect and it quickly becomes clear that Nucky, having recognized the financial opportunity that this new set of circumstances offers him, is chiefly responsible for orchestrating the shipment and supply of alcohol into Atlantic City, New Jersey. In defiance of the Volsted Act and calling those who passed the law "those ignorant bastards," Nucky performs the dual role of corrupt Republican politician and powerful head of an organization of gangsters and bootleggers, as well as appearing to the ordinary citizens as a decent, hard-working, even sympathetic character.

Is Nucky completely to blame for his duplicity and greed? Or is it simply an inevitable and necessary part of living in society?

The Two Faces of Nucky

The character of Nucky is loosely based on the real New Jersey politician Enoch L. Johnson (1883–1968), who acted as Sheriff and County Treasurer of Atlantic City between 1911 and 1941. Like the real figure, Buscemi's character controls and oversees not only the finances of Atlantic City life but also every other aspect in relation to business, leisure, and domestic life.

In the book *Boardwalk Empire: The Birth, High Times, and Corruption of Atlantic City* (2002) on which the television show was initially based, author Nelson Johnson shows that the real Enoch Johnson "established himself as a force in two different worlds. He was both the most powerful Republican in New Jersey, who could influence the destinies of governors and senators, and a racketeer, respected and trusted by organized crime."[1]

Likewise, Buscemi's character is motivated by financial gain and even travels to Belfast in Season Two to sell firearms to the Irish Republican Army in exchange for Irish whiskey which he ships to Atlantic City. His exalted position

---

[1] Nelson Johnson, *Boardwalk Empire: The Birth, High Times, and Corruption of Atlantic City* (Plexus, 2002).

allows him a high level of political influence, enabling him to rig the 1920 election, in which Republican candidate Edward Bader becomes mayor of Atlantic City and Warren Harding becomes US president.

Harding's election ensures that Nucky can forge strong political connections in Washington and receive funding for the highway that he plans to construct in Season Two, from which he hopes to profit. The show makes it very clear that corruption and politics go hand in hand as political figures from both within and outside Atlantic City abuse their positions as they patronize brothels and attend lavish and hedonistic parties.

But there's a more sinister aspect of this corruption and of the character of Nucky. In the pilot, Nucky orders his brother Eli, played by Shea Whigham, Sheriff of Atlantic County, to kill Hans Schroeder, the abusive husband of Irish immigrant Margaret, played by Kelly McDonald, for whom Nucky has developed feelings. As the show progresses and despite his resignation from his position as County Treasurer at the end of Season Two, Nucky becomes increasingly dangerous, continuing to kill his adversaries, including Jimmy in Season Two, whom he kills himself, as well as others including Gyp Rosetti in Season Three.

However, Nucky is embraced and loved by his constituents, as the real Enoch Johnson was, due to his charm, charisma, generous philanthropy. Nelson Johnson recounts that the father of the real Enoch Johnson, "taught his son early on that government and the electoral processes were no more than a game to be mastered for personal power." We recognize this form of manipulation in Season One when Nucky is at the height of his popularity due to his campaigning before the upcoming election. We see that he, as the oldest son of an Irish immigrant, is clearly much loved amongst the Irish community, particularly in "Nights in Ballygran" when he holds his annual Saint Patrick's Day Celtic Dinner for the Ancient Order of the Celts. He is also embraced by the African-American community, through his partnership with bootlegger Chalky White, played by Michael Kenneth Williams, and amongst women, demonstrated through his connection with the aforementioned Women's Temperance League.

In Season Two, even US Assistant Attorney General Esther Randolph, played by Julianne Nicholson, admits that she likes him, despite the fact that she's attempting to prosecute him for election fraud as well as murder and bootlegging ("To the Lost"). In "Bone for Tuna," Nucky is to receive the St. Gregory's award from the Catholic Church for his charitable work and donations; he acts as benefactor and finances the construction of a new wing of a hospital and subsequently has the wing named after him. Throughout the first three seasons, his philanthropy appears from the outside to be altruistic kindness but it is always politically motivated as Nucky continually seeks to manipulate the vote of the ordinary citizens of Atlantic City towards the Republican cause.

In Season Three Nucky has given up his position as County Treasurer and appears to be dedicated exclusively to philanthropy, yet he retains control of the criminal organization. When he proclaims in the first episode of this season, "I'm a philanthropist now," the reply is "You're a gangster. Plain and simple," illustrating the corruption and consequential violence that fundamentally underlies this society.

Subjective Violence

In his book *Violence: Six Sideways Reflections* (2008), controversial philosopher and culture critic Slavoj Žižek argues that violence is a necessary characteristic of Western society, "inherent to this 'normal' state of things"[2] and that it comes in a number of forms with varying degrees of visibility. He argues that there are essentially two forms of violence: subjective and objective, both of which are interconnected and highly significant in *Boardwalk Empire*.

Subjective violence is, according to Žižek at "the forefront of our minds" (p. 1) as it is easily seen, it involves a specific

---

[2] Slavoj Žižek, *Violence: Six Sideways Reflections* (Picador, 2008), p. 2.

violent act, and we can recognize a clear perpetrator. *Boardwalk Empire* is replete with images of subjective violence, between the competing gangsters and bootleggers, which can be clearly seen in the various shootings and the often gory spectacles. Such images include the violence that ensues throughout Season One between Nucky and the Delessio Brothers, throughout Season Two which begins with a shootout between the Ku Klux Klan and Chalky at Chalky's warehouse, ordered by the Commodore, and the highly violent character Gyp Rosetti in Season Three.

Notable instances of subjective violence occur in the Pilot, when violence is inflicted in close-up as Jimmy shoots Arnold Rothstein's man in the head and in "Gimcrack & Bunkum" when Eli kills alderman and ward boss George O' Neill, played by William Hill, by first slitting his throat and then hitting him repeatedly in the head with a wrench, reminiscent of the infamous scene in *Irreversible*. In "The Age of Reason" Jimmy slits the throat of Herman, a man hanging upside down in Manny Horowitz's butcher shop; other murders include that of Angela, played by Aleksa Palladino, and her girlfriend Louise by Manny Horowitz in "Georgia Peaches" and James Neery by Richard Harrow in "To the Lost," as well as Nucky's murder of Jimmy in the same episode. This level of violence continues throughout the show and is also easily seen in the shocking violence of short-tempered Sicilian Gyp Rosetti throughout Season Three. Particularly violent examples include Cousin Franco, whom Rosetti buries neck deep in the sand and then beats violently to death with a shovel to the head in "A Man, A Plan . . ." and the scene where Rosetti burns Sheriff Victor Sickles to death for simply wishing him good luck in "Bone for Tuna."

Objective Violence

Yet subjective violence is just the most visible form and Žižek maintains that spectacles of violence including terrorist attacks and suicide bombings distract us from the objective violence all around us. Objective violence is not as easily seen and is itself divided into two levels: symbolic and systemic. Symbolic violence is contained within our language and communication and involves forms of discrimination including racism and misogyny. In his discussion of the violence of language and the symbolic order, Žižek offers the example of the violence that followed the publication of caricatures of the Prophet Muhammad in the Danish newspaper *Jyllands-Posten* in 2005 and the ensuing "clash of civilisations" that resulted from an increase in global communication. Žižek argues that "A torrent of humiliations and frustrations were condensed into the caricatures. This condensation, it needs to be borne in mind, is a basic fact of language, of constructing and imposing a certain symbolic field" (p. 60). Thus the much publicized clashes, instances of subjective violence, were a product of an underlying objective violence, which was communicated worldwide through images and language.

The second form of objective violence, systemic, lies beneath our language systems and is endemic to our ideology, thus rendering it invisible, although it remains very real. It is "the more subtle forms of coercion that sustain relations of domination and exploitation, including the threat of violence." Systemic violence surrounds us in the everyday but we don't recognize it and we are all complicit in its operation and continuation: "Systemic violence is thus something like the notorious 'dark matter' of physics" (p. 2). It is obscured by subjective violence, thus demonstrating the duplicitous nature of our society and ideology. Žižek exemplifies this underlying level of violence by discussing the example of Russian philosopher Nikolai Lossky, who was forced into exile in 1922 by the Soviet government, after he turned his back on the Russian Orthodox Church and spoke out against post-revolution excesses. Žižek argues that "There was no subjective evil in their life, just the invisible background of this systemic violence" (p. 10), a form of violence that ensures the domination and exploitation of certain members of society. *Boardwalk Empire* fundamentally revolves around the systemic violence of Western ideology and capitalism and exposing the paradoxes of social life.

Žižek fundamentally ties systemic violence with capitalism, arguing: "The notion of objective violence needs to be thoroughly historicized: it took on a new shape with capitalism. Marx described the mad, self-enhancing circulation of capital. . . . Therein resides the fundamental systemic violence of capitalism, much more uncanny than any direct pre-capitalist socio-ideological violence: this violence is no longer attributable to concrete individuals and their "evil" intentions, but is purely "objective," systemic, anonymous" (p. 12). It is the gap between these two poles that Žižek discusses for much of his book, exposing the paradoxes of capitalism and social life. Žižek again employs his "chocolate laxative" metaphor, also used in his article "Nobody Has to Be Vile" (2006) to demonstrate the two-sided and paradoxical nature of social life, ideology, and American capitalism. In that earlier article he argues:

> There is a chocolate-flavoured laxative available on the shelves of US stores which is publicised with the paradoxical injunction: Do you have constipation? Eat more of this chocolate!—i.e. eat more of something that itself causes constipation. The structure of the chocolate laxative can be discerned throughout today's ideological landscape; it is what makes a figure like Soros so objectionable. He stands for ruthless financial exploitation combined with its counter-agent, humanitarian worry about the catastrophic social consequences of the unbridled market economy. . . . We should have no illusions: liberal communists are the enemy of every true progressive struggle today. (*London Review of Books*, 6th April 2006)

The term "liberal communists" refers to "The usual suspects: Bill Gates and George Soros, the CEOs of Google, IBM, Intel, eBay, as well as court-philosophers like Thomas Friedman. The true conservatives today, they argue, are not only the old right, with its ridiculous belief in authority, order, and parochial patriotism, but also the old left, with its war against capitalism: both fight their shadow-theatre battles in disregard of the new realities."

Such philanthropic business magnates embody this paradoxical nature, as Žižek argues: "While they fight subjective violence, liberal communists are the very agents of the structural violence which creates the conditions for the explosions of subjective violence" (*Violence*, p. 36). In "Nobody Has to Be Vile" Žižek maintains that the "two faces of Bill Gates are exactly like the two faces of Soros: on the one hand, a cruel businessman, destroying or buying out competitors, aiming at a virtual monopoly; on the other, the great philanthropist who makes a point of saying: "What does it serve to have computers if people do not have enough to eat?" This is an argument that he returns to in *Violence*, arguing that "In liberal communist ethics, the ruthless pursuit of profit is counteracted by charity. Charity is the humanitarian mask hiding the face of economic exploitation," a statement that can also be applied to Nucky's contradictory public image.

Blood in Our Faces

Of these two forms of violence, *Boardwalk Empire* has been most criticized for its instances of extreme abject violence. Matt Zoller Seitz points out that acts of violence play, "like textbook examples of a show trying to jack up its excitement level with 'Oh my God, I can't believe they did that!' mayhem."[3] Zoller Seitz holds that such images of violence "were shocking, not because they came out of nowhere, but because they cheerfully confirmed the show's allegiance to the worst impulses of Martin Scorsese and *The Sopranos*—the tendency to spotlight pissing-contest behavior between macho guys in the most gruesome terms imaginable."

In a similar vein, Greg Braxton writes that "The Prohibition-era mobster tale *Boardwalk Empire*, which received eighteen Emmy nominations this year, has featured a close-up of a man getting his head caved in by a heavy wrench, the scalping of a veteran of the American-Indian Wars, and the

---

[3] Matt Zoller Seitz, "'Boardwalk Empire' Takes a Cartoonish Turn," *Salon.com* (24th October 2011).

slaying of a man hanging upside down in a butcher shop pleading for his life before getting his throat sliced open with a freshly sharpened blade."[4]

What's significant about these types of reactions is that such critics focus on the subjective visual violence of the show and not the system of underlying violence that causes and facilitates such images, demonstrating Žižek's argument that objective violence occurs under the surface and goes largely unnoticed, whilst subjective violence becomes spectacle and comes to the fore. Such strong violence has become stereotypically tied with HBO since its first broadcast in the 1970s. With its tagline "It's Not TV, It's HBO" the network distinguished itself as different and superior to everything else from the very beginning. It was "Quality TV," which challenged genre conventions and audience expectations and thus used violence in a very different way than audiences had become accustomed to.

Images of subjective violence also featured heavily in shows including *Oz* and *The Sopranos*. But what distinguishes *Boardwalk Empire* from older HBO shows is its extremely high production values, with the pilot—directed by Martin Scorsese, who continues to act as an executive producer—reportedly being the most expensive pilot ever produced for TV, at eighteen million dollars. In the pilot, Scorsese establishes the show's visual flamboyance and its often frenetic pacing using his anachronistic camerawork and editing techniques including rapid montages, quick zooms towards characters, and tight close-ups.

The show was created by Terence Winter, once a writer for *The Sopranos* and is executive-produced by Mark Wahlberg, demonstrating the increasing move of directors, producers, and stars from cinema to big budget TV shows and miniseries. Such visual stylization and decadence significantly also serves to disguise the systemic violence at the heart of the wealth enjoyed by Nucky and several other main

---

[4] Greg Braxton, "Extreme Violence Cuts Bloody Path through Noteworthy TV Dramas," *Los Angeles Times* (10th November 2011).

characters, as the audience often becomes engrossed in the beauty of this decadent world.

Happy Endings?

Towards the end of his study of violence, Žižek comments on the danger of habit, arguing that "Habits are the very stuff our identities are made of. In them, we enact and thus define what we effectively are as social beings, often in contrast with our perception of what we are. In their transparency they are the medium of social violence" (*Violence*, p. 164). He asks "Isn't this how ideology works? The explicit ideological text or practice is sustained by an unplayed series of obscene superego supplements" (p. 170). *Boardwalk Empire* allows us to see through the socially accepted norms of ideology and to recognize the violence that underlies the capitalist system through the show's images of subjective violence, as well as its exposure of the objective, systemic violence that sustains the capitalist system both in 1920s New Jersey and similarly in society today. Nucky Thompson personifies this concept of the paradox of capitalism.

Ultimately, what the show highlights is that violence exists everywhere in this society: the first three seasons demonstrate that despite several attempts being made on his life, Nucky remains somewhat untouchable, protected by the capitalism that supports systemic violence, a fact that is alluded to in the show's opening credit sequence. The opening credits illustrate this sense of contradiction between Nucky's public and private lives and his mastery of his dual roles. Nucky walks onto the beach on a sunny, peaceful day; from the beginning he is portrayed as an authoritative, solitary figure, silhouetted against the sea and sky. There are close-ups of his eyes, symbolic of his authority and surveillance of Atlantic City, his red boutonniere, the symbol of his flamboyance and class consciousness, and his gold cigarette case, another material representation of his financial status, and a representation of the materialism of capitalism.

As soon as unopened whiskey bottles begin to wash ashore, the sky suddenly turns darker and the sea stormier as bottles begin to break against the boardwalk and the sea envelops his feet. The weather again changes to become calm, representing the interchanging and merging nature of his various roles and indicating the untouchable nature of the character who is not affected or dirtied by the swell of the tide or the sudden rough weather. The credits end as he retreats unaffected, striding towards his empire. Buscemi's period costume clashes with the anachronistically employed rock music, illustrating that this show will consciously emphasize contradictions. This opening music is in stark contrast to the exclusively Ragtime soundtrack that features in every episode and the show has no customized score, instead using pre-existing Jazz Age music.

Only time will tell whether justice will prevail and whether Nucky will eventually be reprimanded or killed. Whatever happens, Žižek's concept of systemic violence will permeate all echelons of society, as it still does today.

15
The Stories Some People Tell

CAM COBB

The second scene of *Boardwalk Empire* opens with Nucky Thompson, treasurer of Atlantic City, delivering a speech. With gravity, he sets the scene as follows: "Years ago, there was a young boy who lived in this very city. The winter of eighty-eight, some of you remember, a blizzard of biblical proportions." Speaking at a rally on the eve of Prohibition, Nucky continues his tale: "A family was snowbound, freezing, without food or heat. The father vanished, laid to waste by alcohol. And so it was left to this boy, this little man of tender years to fend for himself and his family." Detailing a harrowing journey, Nucky states: "Off in the cold he went, worn shoes, wrapped in rags, newspaper lining his thin wool coat, as he trudged chest-deep in snow to the rail yard, foraging on hands and bloody knees for scraps."

Nucky's audience, a group of the Women's Temperance League, are visibly moved by this story. But there is more. Nucky goes on to explain that when the boy was unable to find food, "he took a broom handle and in desperation killed his family's dinner. Three wharf rats hiding in the hold of a ship." Members of the audience gasp. And after a brief pause Nucky reveals that he is in fact the little boy from the story, which prompts a healthy applause.

But Nucky's story has a surprising epilogue. Shortly after exiting the meeting, he confides to his trusted protégé,

Jimmy Darmody: "First rule of politics kiddo, never let the truth get in the way of a good story." *Boardwalk Empire* is a vast narrative filled with characters who themselves tell one another stories. And in sharing stories, these characters tell outright lies and half-truths.

The End Hasn't Come Yet

Because narrative interlocks with storytelling I will begin by asking: What's in a story? According to Carola Conle, stories demonstrate five core components, including: a temporal sequence, a plot, a set of characters, a context, and, ultimately a sense of ending.[1]

Boardwalk Empire has the first four of these five components.

- **The events portrayed in the series follow a forward moving timeline set in the 1920s.**

- **The plot depicts a chain of events centered on the criminal and political happenings in Atlantic City. More precisely, the plot focuses on the ongoing struggle for power within and around the city.**

- **A group of characters, directly or indirectly linked to this power struggle, occupy the landscape of the story.**

- **A variety of contextual factors relating to 1920s America, such as the women's right movement, racism, anti-Semitism, Prohibition, and government and police corruption contribute to the milieu of *Boardwalk Empire*.**

If we accept Conle's definition of a story, then we might say that *Boardwalk Empire* is an unfinished story, because

----

[1] Carola Conle, "An Anatomy of Narrative Curricula," *Educational Researcher* (2003), pp. 3–15.

at present the series lacks a sense of ending. As Nucky says to Margaret in the second season, "The end hasn't come yet."

Never Let Happening Truth Get in the Way of a Good Story Truth

Assuming we agree that *Boardwalk Empire* is, at least for the time being, an unfinished story, to what extent might we say it's a true story? For this chapter, I will broadly define *story truth* as an experience derived from a story and *happening truth* as a literal depiction of historical and/or current events.[2] With these two terms in mind, let's return to the matter of the storytelling.

While stories might depict facts taken from current or past events, they don't always portray those facts with complete accuracy. So what are the implications? If I were to tell you a disparaging story about one of your friends that blended fact with fiction how would you be able to distinguish between the two? Would it matter whether the story was entertaining?

The tension between story truth and happening truth has interested philosophers for thousands of years. In the *Republic*, which to a large extent is about education, Plato asked, "Aren't there two kinds of story, one true and the other false?" In addressing this question, Plato cautioned educators about narratives that depict story truth and he went as far as to decree that, "Whether in epic, lyric, or tragedy, a god must always be represented as he is."

While the writers of *Boardwalk Empire* technically do not break Plato's rule, they do make extensive use of story truth. Nucky Thompson, for instance, is a fictional construct. While much of his character is based on Enoch Johnson, who *was* the treasurer of Atlantic City, Nucky remains an example of story truth. But why place fictional characters alongside his-

---

[2] Cathy Coulter, Charles Michael, and Leslie Poynor, "Storytelling as Pedagogy: An Unexpected Outcome of Narrative Inquiry," *Curriculum Inquiry*, (2007), pp. 103–122.

torical figures, such as Al Capone and Arnold Rothstein? Perhaps the writers of *Boardwalk Empire* subscribe to Nucky's own credo, "Never let the truth get in the way of a good story."

Fishing in the Pool of Declarative Memory

While *story truth* and *happening truth* help inform us about the content of narratives, they do not tell us *how* narratives are constructed. To better understand what it is we do when we tell stories we need to ask: What's involved in forming a narrative?

According to Paul Hazel we draw from our declarative memory when we compose narratives. Our declarative memory is "memory for things, events, and experiences that we are able to consciously access and articulate."[3] Two key aspects contribute to our declarative memory, namely episodic memory and semantic memory.[4] In developing episodic memory we draw from our own personal experiences, and we use semantic memory to store information and knowledge about our surrounding world.[5]

The way we form narratives thus draws from different parts and activities of the brain. Our hippocampus helps us to encode spatial and time-based experiences while our frontal lobes help us to then draw from those memories as we use language, make decisions, solve problems, and socialize. Ultimately, in a strictly biological sense, we might say that narrative arises from "the interaction between the hippocampus and the frontal lobes."

But narrative is more than an interaction between two parts of the human brain. It is also a process that helps us

---

[3] Peter Hazel, "Toward a Narrative Pedagogy for Interactive Learning Environments," *Interactive Learning Environments* (2008), p. 201.

[4] Larry R. Squire, "Memory Systems of the Brain: A Brief History and Current Perspective," *Neurobiology of Learning and Memory* (2004), pp. 171–77.

[5] Neil Burgess, Eleanor A. Maguire, and John O'Keefe, "The Human Hippocampus and Spatial and Episodic Memory," *Neuron* (2002), pp. 625–641.

to reflect, express ourselves, interact with others, and, ultimately, construct identity. In sharing stories we meditate on our past experiences and form a *life script*. Constructing and telling stories about our past helps us to better understand what we have experienced and believed, as well as what sorts of implications are associated with these memories. Of course, narrative isn't strictly about looking into the past. In some circumstances we use our life stories to draw conclusions about the present or the future.

Bookcases and Billiard Balls

Atlantic City racketeer Chalky White intermingles declarative memory with memory-oriented sense making when interrogating a member of the Ku Klux Klan. The scene occurs in the fourth episode of the series, entitled "Anastasia." Prior to the interrogation Chalky's driver, Kendall, was murdered by two Philadelphia bootleggers. The bootleggers staged the crime scene to look like a lynching in an effort to ignite racial tension in Atlantic City.

To avert social unrest a local leader of the Ku Klux Clan is brought into custody and, Chalky, a prominent member of the city's African-American community, is given an opportunity to interrogate him. But rather than opening with a series of questions Chalky shares a story. He begins by describing his father's work as a carpenter. He goes on to explain how his father came to build a vast library for Theo Purcell, a wealthy man in his hometown. Shortly after completing the library another man, posing as a potential customer, lured Chalky's father to the edge of town where he was hanged from a pepper tree. When he finishes his story Chalky carefully opens a case that contains a set of tools. He tells the suspect that the tools once belonged to his father. "What are you gonna do with them?" the suspect asks. Believing that Kendall was lynched, Chalky's story links the past to the present. In sharing this story Chalky makes a personal connection to the interrogation, stresses the gravity of the situation, and ultimately conveys his disgust with the racism that pervades his world.

New York City gangster Arnold Rothstein exhibits a variety of narrative processes in the second episode of the series. As the scene opens, Rothstein is playing billiards in a lavishly decorated room in New York City. Interrupting the game, Lucky Luciano ushers Frankie Yale into the room. Rothstein then shares a story from his past. He tells Yale that he once knew a man who "made a comfortable living wagering whether or not he could swallow certain objects, billiard balls being his specialty." Rothstein proceeds to recall an evening he challenged the man to a wager. "Ten thousand to do the trick with the billiard ball of my choosing," he said.

The man choked to death on the spot Rothstein bluntly confides, and he then goes on to explain that the cue ball he selected was actually one-sixteenth of an inch larger than the other balls. "The moral of this story," Rothstein concludes, "is that if I'd cause a stranger to choke to death for my own amusement what do you think I'd do to you if you don't tell me who ordered you to kill Colosimo?"

Assuming this is an actual event from Rothstein's past, the story exemplifies how episodic memory can be used to recall events and formulate personal narratives. But the vignette isn't purely a matter of recall. Rothstein is also telling a violent story from his past to indicate that he's a dangerous man, and will continue to be one in the foreseeable future. Because the story acts as a threat to Frankie Yale's wellbeing, we might say that Rothstein's narrative is used to draw conclusions about the present as well as the future. And for Frankie these conclusions present rather unpleasant possibilities.

Rothstein's billiard ball narrative is more than a matter of episodic memory recall and using stories to draw conclusions. It's also about identity. When we draw from our life stories to make a point, whatever the point is, we're using the narrative mode not only to express ourselves, but also to converse with others. While our life stories help us to draw conclusions about the past, present, and future they also help us to sculpt our own identity.

In sharing a violent story from his past, Rothstein shapes his image in the eyes Frankie Yale and Lucky Luciano. It's an image of ruthlessness and power. In constructing identity, we select from our own reservoir of memories and then shape and package those memories into life stories. And in a much broader sense, we use the narrative mode as a form of reflection, expression, interaction, and identity construction. While Rothstein's billiard ball story might on the surface seem to be a straightforward anecdote, it exemplifies all four of these narrative processes.

Pedagogues at Large

Like narrative, pedagogy is a word that means different things to different people. When discussing pedagogy, philosophers and educational theorists tend to focus, but certainly not agree, on a broad range of ideas. We'll look at three core aspects of pedagogy: [6]

1. **Pedagogy is an exchange that involves reasoning**

2. **Pedagogy is an educative exchange between adults and children, and**

3. **The practice of pedagogy is reflective.**

So, first, pedagogy is not a one-sided experience. It's an exchange of ideas where people have an opportunity to share, and reason out their views. Socrates, for instance, used such words as *interview* and *converse* to describe his own learning exchanges in his Euthyphro and Crito. Nearly twenty-four centuries later, in *Pedagogy of the Oppressed*, Brazilian activist and educator Paulo Freire argued that "Without dialogue there is no communication, and without communication there can be no true education."[7]

For pedagogical exchanges to occur, the space within which ideas are being shared and conclusions are being

---

[6] Max van Manen, "Pedagogy, Virtue, and Narrative Identity in Teaching," *Curriculum Inquiry* (1994), pp. 135–170.

[7] Paulo Freire, *Pedagogy of the Oppressed* (Continuum, 2000), pp. 92–93.

drawn needs to be safe, in both a physical and emotional sense. Let's return to Rothstein's billiard ball story. As a pedagogue, Rothstein tells the story to Frankie Yale in the presence of Lucky Luciano. Luciano is a gangster on Rothstein's payroll. The room presumably belongs to Rothstein, and one might reasonably expect that other employees are situated outside the room. For Frankie Yale, the space is neither physically nor emotionally safe. In terms of fostering a safe learning space, we could conclude that Rothstein falls short as a pedagogue. But does he succeed on other counts?

After completing his anecdote, Rothstein asks Yale to explain the moral of the story. In posing this question he's inviting Yale to reason out possible implications of the story. Viewing the story on a literal level Yale comments on the danger of trying to swallow billiard balls. And while Frankie Yale fails to identify the deeper implications of the story, he *was* given an opportunity—albeit one that involved duress— to formulate and share his interpretation. Rothstein responds to Yale's conclusion by putting forward his own idea of the moral of the story. While the exchange between Rothstein and Yale is brief, it's an exchange that involves reasoning, and on this count we could argue that Rothstein, at least in part, fosters a pedagogical experience.

Second, pedagogy is unique in that it involves a learning exchange between adults and children. While not everyone holds this view, those who *do* assert that pedagogical experiences are strictly ones that help children and youths to mature. In his *On Education*, Immanuel Kant suggested that, "on the whole we should try to draw out their own ideas, founded on reason."[8] He went on to argue that, "When the child is set free he soon recovers his sense of natural elasticity."

In order to foster a blend of learning and maturing in children and youths, pedagogues must not only be aware of the interests and needs of those they are teaching, but also of the intricacies of child and youth development. Those who hold this view of pedagogy define *adult-adult* learning ex-

---

[8] Immanuel Kant, *On Education* (Dover), p. 81.

changes as andragogy. But not everyone holds this view. According to Max van Manen writers in the Americas tend to use pedagogy in a more general sense-one that is inclusive of adult-adult learning exchanges.

In drawing from his experiences with *both* adult and child learners, Freire used the word pedagogy in the broader sense in his own writing. According to Freire, pedagogical exchanges occur when students become "critical co-investigators in dialogue with the teacher." And, with this definition in mind, we could conclude that Nucky's wharf rat story and Rothstein's billiard ball story both represent pedagogical moments. While both Rothstein and Nucky make use of the narrative mode to facilitate learning experiences, their practice of pedagogy is limited. In Rothstein's case there is a pesky specter of domination lurking beneath the surface, and in Nucky's situation there is a distinct lack of dialogue.

Third, pedagogy is rooted in reflection. Pedagogues pose questions, not only to learners but also to themselves. And these questions are meant to foster critical thinking. For one to thoughtfully facilitate an exchange and reasoning out of ideas, one needs to address a variety of questions, such as: What is being examined? Why is this matter being examined? How do I view it? What sort of evidence supports my view? How do others view this matter? What sort of evidence supports their view?

In over twenty dialogues Socrates demonstrates this question-and-answer process to examine such topics as justice, love, virtue, and the afterlife. In *Euthyphro*, for instance, he converses with Euthyphro to inquire into the nature of piety. As a pedagogue, Socrates poses questions to identify what exactly is the matter at hand (piety), how they view this matter (or particular aspects of it), and what sort of evidence supports or refutes their observations. In a very general sense, Socrates and Euthyphro put forward and then question a variety of truth claims about how we are to define piety. And while Socrates is certainly a proficient questioner, he isn't the only one. Whether someone is teaching kindergarten or conversing with a colleague at work, question posing, or as Paulo Freire calls it, "problem-posing," is a part of a pedagogue's reflective thinking. And the actions of Nucky, Chalky, and Rothstein hint at this process in *Boardwalk Empire*.

In composing his wharf rat story, Nucky might have asked himself a number of reflective questions, such as, 1. How appropriate is this story for the context of the rally? 2. What sorts of lessons could be drawn from this story? 3. What do these messages say about Prohibition, the topic at hand?

Chalky too might have pondered a variety of questions before stepping into the interrogation room, including: 1. How will I interview this suspect? 2. Which personal story, if any, should I share? 3. What will my story say about the situation at hand?

Similarly, before meeting with Frankie Yale, Rothstein might have asked himself, 1. What am I going to say? 2. How am I going to say it? 3. What sorts of messages will my words convey? Rather than directly threatening Yale when he entered into the room Rothstein chose to tell a story. And this story doesn't seem to have been selected randomly.

Nucky, Chalky, and Rothstein, we might conclude, are all reflective pedagogues. But, given what we know about narrative and pedagogy, how should we define narrative pedagogy?

Do You Want to Know What the Moral of This Tale Is, Mr. Yale?

Stories can help us to better understand and *read* our experiences, as well as our surroundings.[9] "A story is a beautiful means of teaching religion, values, history, traditions, and customs; a creative method of introducing characters and places; an imaginative way to instill hope and resourceful thinking." In a broad sense we might say that narrative ped-

---

[9] Kieran Egan, *Teaching as Storytelling: An Alternative Approach to Teaching and Curriculum in the Elementary School* (University of Chicago Press, 1989).

agogy blends storytelling with the aims and practices of pedagogy. But it's more than that. Narrative pedagogy is also a matter of interpretive thinking and collaborating.[10]

First, narrative pedagogy encourages interpretive thinking. To facilitate this active thought process, pedagogues refrain from "focusing on content, facts, figures, and abstract concepts" and instead pose larger questions about the narrative at hand.[11] The narrative itself might stem from an experience lived by the pedagogue. It might also stem from an experience lived by one, or more, of the students. It might even stem from a past experience shared between the pedagogue and the students. And the questions that are posed about the narrative are critical ones. These questions beckon students to view the narrative from multiple perspectives, challenge previously held assumptions, and ultimately, use the narrative to draw new conclusions about the world. These queries also invite students to reflect on their own reasoning process. As an experience then, narrative pedagogy presents a way of shifting attention from memorization and the receiving of information, to reasoning. In this way, storytelling can become a means to *discover* rather than *purely accumulate* knowledge.

Let's return to Arnold Rothstein and the billiard ball story. After sharing his personal narrative, Rothstein invites (or pressures) Frankie Yale to reflect on the story, by asking: "Do you know what the moral is of this tale, Mr. Yale?" He is actually posing two important questions to Frankie: What does this story mean *to you*? And what does this story mean *for us*? Both questions present an opportunity for Frankie to consider the events of the narrative as well as their

---

[10] Pamela M. Ironside, "Using Narrative Pedagogy: Learning and Practicing Interpretive Thinking," *Issues and Innovations in Nursing Education* (2006), pp. 478–486.

[11] Catherine A. Andrews, Pamela M. Ironside, Catherine Nosek, Sharon L. Sims, Melinda M. Swenson, Christine Yeomans, Patricia K. Young, and Nancy Diekelmann, "Enacting Narrative Pedagogy: The Lived Experiences of Students and Teachers," *Nursing and Health Care Perspectives* (2001), p. 257.

implications. They also challenge Frankie to reason out his interpretation of the story's meaning. And while Frankie interprets the billiard ball story in a literal way, the situation itself remains one of narrative pedagogy. Rothstein presented a personal narrative and then posed a question, which led to a brief, but reasoned exchange. Because the scene ends after Rothstein shares his own view of the story we do not know how the conversation ultimately unfolded.

When practicing narrative pedagogy, interpretive thinking is encouraged within a collaborative dynamic. Although we find *personal* meanings and significances in the narratives we encounter, we also communicate—and, at times co-construct—those meanings and significances with others. Pamela Ironside has described this narrative-based interplay between teachers and students—and/or among students—as "converging conversations." Within a collaborative dynamic, according to Paulo Freire: "The students—no longer docile listeners—are now critical co-investigators in dialogue with the teacher. The teacher presents the material to the students for their consideration, and re-considers her earlier considerations as the students express their own." But if we are to say that Rothstein and Yale are critical co-investigators, could we say the same for Nucky and the audience at the rally? Let's return to the scene that opened this chapter, the second scene of *Boardwalk Empire*.

Wharf Rats and Pedagogy

By detailing a young boy's harrowing journey, Nucky shares a personal narrative with the Women's Temperance League. Although his wharf rat story isn't actually true, as Nucky privately admits to Jimmy, it does convey story truth. And, at least according to Carola Conle's definition, it *is* a complete story, presenting a temporal sequence, a plot, set of characters, context, and sense of ending.

Nucky's story, told on the very eve of prohibition, presents an *opportunity* for his audience, his students, to reflect on the young boy's predicament and relate it to their own lives as well as to their social context. But instead of posing questions Nucky follows the story by explaining what it means to him, and then promptly leaves the rally. Because Nucky does not use his communal space to foster dialogue, and because he does not challenge his students to critically examine the narrative at hand, the wharf rat story does not *fully* represent practice of narrative pedagogy. Similarly, Chalky does not pose questions in what we see of his interrogation. And while they might be crooks, cheats and racketeers, Nucky, Chalky, and Rothstein are all, in their own ways, narrative pedagogues at large.

The Bootleggers

CHELSI BARNARD ARCHIBALD holds a Masters of Arts in English from Weber State University. She writes television recaps for Socialite Life, a prominent celebrity gossip blog. When she isn't analyzing the underground world of Atlantic City, she can be found wearing top and tails at Babette's Supper Club, singing like Marlene Dietrich, and drinking champagne from the bottle.

NEIL BAKER recently completed his Bachelor of Arts at Hope International University and plans to begin law school soon. Neil started his schooling with the goal of becoming a Christian minister; but after getting involved with a few too many religious groups with people like Agent Van Alden, he decided to go a different way. Maybe God will forgive him. (On second thought, if God's temperament is anything like what Van Alden seems to think it is, maybe not.)

PATRICIA BRACE is a Professor of Art History at Southwest Minnesota State University, in Marshall, Minnesota. Her research and writing is focused on aesthetics and popular culture. Her studio work is in jewelry design and many new pieces in her spring show were inspired by the time she spent this year in the *Boardwalk Empire* era. Pat would love to meet Richard Harrow to discuss the aesthetic meaning of his collages and admire his guns. . . .

ROD CARVETH is an Assistant Professor in the Department of Communication Studies at Morgan State University. The grand-nephew of a real-life Depression-era bootlegger, Rod is currently working on the biography of Chalkie White. You should find it under the "Truthiness" section of your local bookstore sometime in the near future.

CAM COBB uses personal stories in his teaching, although his narratives don't include billiards or bookcases. And while he does live in Canada, Cam's stories surprisingly never seem to involve any blizzards. Cam is an Assistant Professor at the University of Windsor, and he's another narrative pedagogue at large.

MICHAEL DA SILVA wrote his chapter while pursuing graduate studies in legal philosophy in the Rutgers University's New Brunswick-based Department of Philosophy. Despite his proximity to Atlantic City, he respects Nucky Thompson's turf and accordingly has yet to step foot on the boardwalk. He previously contributed to a pop culture and philosophy collection devoted to *Arrested Development* and has co-authored chapters in collections on *30 Rock* and *The Walking Dead*.

DON FALLIS is Professor of Information Resources and Adjunct Professor of Philosophy at the University of Arizona. He has written several philosophy articles on lying and deception, including "What Is Lying?" in the *Journal of Philosophy* and "The Most Terrific Liar You Ever Saw in Your Life" in *The Catcher in the Rye and Philosophy: A Book for Bastards, Morons, and Madmen*. Although he has played Monopoly many times, he has only visited Atlantic City once. Disappointingly, there was no trauma, there was no blood.

JOHN FITZPATRICK teaches philosophy at the University of Tennessee at Chattanooga. He received a PhD in Philosophy from the main branch of the University of Tennessee in Knoxville in 2001. He is the author of *John Stuart Mill's Political Philosophy: Balancing Freedom and the Collective Good* (2006), and *Starting with Mill* (2010). He has written several essays on philosophy and popular culture. He has no clear idea of what the state of nature is like, but assumes it is likely to be better than his current circumstances.

RICHARD GREENE is a Professor of Philosophy at Weber State University. He also serves as Executive Chair of the Intercollegiate Ethics Bowl. He's co-edited a number of books on pop culture and philosophy including *Dexter and Philosophy*, *Quentin Tarantino and Philosophy*, and *The Sopranos and Philosophy*. He initially agreed to take on this project when he thought it was about Bored Walk

Umpire—the scintillating story of a major league umpire who experiences such debilitating ennui that he can no longer call strikes.

Ron Hirschbein's Syracuse social science PhD led to his immersion in war and peace studies. He initiated such a program at California State University, Chico, and it survives to this day—despite the fussy academic bureaucracy. He is the author of *Massing the Tropes: The Metaphorical Construction of American Nuclear Strategy* (2005) and *Voting Rights: The Devolution of American Politics* (1999) and has had visiting professorships in peace and conflict studies at University of California campuses in Berkeley and San Diego, and the UN University. Kierkegaard talked of a pessimistic moment: war and peace studies gave him pessimistic decades. So . . . he took a break, indulged in not-so-guilty pleasures and wrote for various philosophy and popular culture series. He's mocked nuclear strategists, bled vampires for what they're worth, and imagined watching *Boardwalk* with Freud. Currently, he works online vexing Walden University's graduate students.

Maria Kingsbury is a librarian at Southwest Minnesota State University and a PhD candidate in rhetoric and technical communication at Texas Tech. When she's not reading and writing—or helping others find things to read and write about—she can often be found with her husband brewing beer and making wine in their home. She's proud to be carrying on the rebellious spirit of the Prohibition brewers and vintners—though the lack of Feds poking around has made it lose some of its spark. . . .

Greg Littmann is Associate Professor of Philosophy at SIUE. By day, he teaches critical thinking, philosophy of mind, metaphysics, and epistemology. By night, he smuggles philosophy out of academia and onto the streets where it belongs, in violation of the unofficial twenty-eighth amendment of the US Constitution prohibiting consumption of philosophy by the public. He has published in metaphysics and the philosophy of logic and has written seventeen chapters for books relating philosophy to popular culture, including volumes on *Breaking Bad, Doctor Who, Game of Thrones, Sons of Anarchy, The Big Bang Theory*, and *The Walking Dead*. If Greg Littmann was a gangster from the 1920s, his nickname would be either "Fuzz-face," "Nose-face," "Fat Greggie," or "Gucky Littmann."

DEBORAH MELLAMPHY is a part-time Assistant Lecturer and Tutor in Film Studies in the School of English, University College Cork, Ireland. In her spare time she is the CEO of Feeney's Irish Oats, based in Belfast. Her research focuses both on videogames and on gender transgression, star theory, and collective authorship in contemporary American cinema. Her teaching interests include the horror genre, gender studies, and film theory. Deborah supplements her income through the use of the empty fish bowl that she leaves in a closely guarded room.

RACHEL ROBISON-GREENE is a PhD Candidate in Philosophy at UMass Amherst. She is co-editor of *The Golden Compass and Philosophy: God Bites the Dust* and *Dexter and Philosophy: Mind over Spatter*. She has contributed chapters to *Quentin Tarantino and Philosophy*, *The Legend of Zelda and Philosophy*, *Zombies, Vampires, and Philosophy*, and *The Walking Dead and Philosophy*. Rachel learned the hard way not to enter into an economic arrangement with Agent Van Alden.

WIELAND SCHWANEBECK is a loyal Hun who occasionally goes to his office at Dresden University of Technology (Germany) to get some sleep. Born in the former GDR, Wieland has had plenty of first-hand experience with rigged elections and smuggling. A teetotaler by choice, he has been a source of embarrassment for his wine-loving parents, which is why he recently tried to make amends and finished his PhD project on the role of impostors and con men in American literature and film. He'd like to be more efficient doing research on his fields of interest (which include gender and masculinity studies, British Film, and the campus novel), but it's the lack of attention to detail that's killing him.

ROBERTO SIRVENT is Associate Professor of Political and Social Ethics at Hope International University. He is co-editor of *By Faith and Reason: The Essential Keith Ward*. Roberto has many friends like Agent Van Alden. They all think Roberto is a heretic, and his contribution to this book only proves their point. He never knows how to respond when his friends say they're praying for him.

Index

"A Man, A Plan . . ." (episode), 183

Abolitionist Movement, xi

Abrahamic religions, 85

absurd hero, 138–141

absurdity, 132, 134, 138–141

active euthanasia. *See* euthanasia

aesthetics, xii

"The Age of Reason" (episode), 82–83, 85, 87, 183

Aked, Charles F., 122, 122n

Alcatraz, 22

alcohol, 6, 18, 31, 54, 76, 105, 122, 125, 133, 140, 143, 146, 155, 162, 179, 191

All the President's Men (movie), 78

American Founding Fathers, 63

American Gothic (painting), 36, 123

American Legion, 62

American-Indian Wars, 186

Amerika (television miniseries), 78

"Anastasia" (episode), 9, 118, 127, 159, 162, 170, 195

Anastasia of Russia, 109

"An Anatomy of Narrative Curricula" (Conle), 192n

Ancient Order of the Celts, 181

Anderson, Hans Christian, 59

Andrews, Catherine A., 201n

Anglo-Irish Treaty, 73–74

Anselmi, Albert, 15

Anti-Saloon League, 122

Anti-Semitism, 192

Aquinas, Thomas, 81

Archibald, Chelsi Barnard, xii, 205

Argonne Forest, 131

Argument of Opposites, 174–75

Aristotle, 48

  friendship, 57, 61

  Golden Mean, 49, 54

  Nicomachean Ethics, 47–48, 54–55, 61

  notion of happiness, xii, 47–51, 53–61, 63

  virtues, 54–55, 57–58, 61

Arminius, Jacobus, 83–84

Arminianism, 84

Artimus Club, 172

Atlantic City, xi, xiii, 6, 9, 11,
17, 19–20, 23, 28–29, 47,
49–50, 57, 60, 62, 69–78,
91, 101–02, 105, 107–08,
113, 117–19, 121, 123,
126–27, 134–35, 140, 148,
152, 168, 180–82, 188,
191–93, 195
Atlantic City Republican
Organization, 11
Atlantic City War Memorial,
103, 141
Atlantic County, 69, 181
Augustine, 81
De Mendacio, 102

Babbitt (Lewis), 42
Babette's Supper Club, 28,
49
bad faith, 135–38, 156, 163
Bader, Ed, 121, 180–81
Baker, Neil, xii, 205
Bailey, Temple, 59
Baptist community, 124
Baseball, 8
"Battle of the Century"
(episode), 73
Baum, L. Frank, 51
Beauvoir, Simone de, 130,
156–59, 161–63
The Ethics of Ambiguity,
155
The Second Sex, 155, 157n
beer, 122, 207
Belfast, 180
"Belle Femme" (episode), 18,
102–04, 108, 159
Benatar, David, 98–99
Bentham, Jeremy, 144
"The Best You Could Do Is Not
Lose" (episode), 163

*Beyond Control: The Amy
Fisher Story* (television
movie), 67
The Bible (book), 41
"Blue Bell Boy" (episode), 81
"Boardwalk Empire" (pilot
episode), 17, 23, 68–69, 71,
108, 112, 120, 125, 179,
181, 183, 187
Boardwalk Empire (television
series):
fans of boardwalk Empire, 36
for episodes, see under title
of episode
historical accuracy, 69–70
*Boardwalk Empire: The Birth,
High Times, and Corruption
of Atlantic City* (Johnson),
16, 16n, 18, 69, 75, 180,
180n
"Boardwalk Empire Re-Cap,
Oedipus Wrecks" (Polay),
43n
"Boardwalk Empire Takes a
Cartoonish turn" (Seitz),
186n
Body Politic, 118–128
Bok, Sissela:
*Lying: Moral choice in Public
and Private* Life, 107–08,
110–11
Bolshevik Revolution, 108
"Bone for Tuna" (episode), 182,
183
Book of Revelation, 41
bootlegging, xii, 6, 25, 30, 72,
101–04, 107, 151, 180,
182–183, 195
Brace, Patricia, xii, 205
Braxton, Greg, 186–87, 187n
Britain, 102
British Government, 70, 73

Broadway, 19
"Broadway Limited" (episode),
9, 109, 160
Brooklyn, 13, 16
The Brothers Karamazov
(Dostoyevsky), 45
Bureau of Internal Revenue,
29
Bureau of Prohibition, 133
Burgess, Neil, 194n
Burns, Ken, 105
Buscemi, Steve, 74, 125,
179–180, 189

Café Beaux Arts, 170
Calvin, John, 81, 81n, 82–83
Calvinism, 84
Camus, Albert, 130, 132, 134,
137
The Myth of Sisyphus, 132,
138
The Stranger, 138–39, 141
Capone, Alphonse (Scarface
Al), xi, xii, 3, 6, 8, 11–13,
15–18, 20, 21–23, 28–29,
31, 59, 70–71, 77, 101–02,
108, 140, 145, 194
Capone, Sonny 72
Carr, Albert Z., 109
"Is Business Bluffing Ethical?"
109
Carthage by the Sea, 127
Carveth, Rod, xii, 205
Catholic Church, 144, 182
Catholicism, 144
Caulfield, Holden, 43
Cheney, Dick, 148
Chicago, 3, 6, 9, 12–13, 18, 21,
60, 71–72, 102, 121, 123
Chicago Tribune (newspaper),
21

Christ, Jesus. *See* Jesus of
Nazareth
Christian values, 179
Christianity, 26, 36, 133–34
Cicero, 126
Pro Murena, 118
Cicero, Illinois, 127
Clarke, Jack, 108
Clarkson (agent), 79, 81, 83–85
Cobb, Cam, xii, 206
Coen Brothers, 125
Colbert, Stephen, 78
Collins, Michael, 70, 73
Colosimo, James (Diamond
Jim), 6, 8, 15, 70, 72, 121,
196
The Commission, 13
the Commodore. *See* Kaestner,
Louis (Commodore)
Coney Island, 6
Congress, 143
Conle, Carola, 192, 192n, 202
consequentialism, 145
The Copacabana (nightclub),
20
Corleone, Michael, 42
Cosa Nostra, 8, 13
Coulter, Cathy, 193n
Cousin Franco, 183
Curriculum, Inquiry, 193n,
197n

D'Alessio, Ignatius, 62, 149,
183
D'Alessio, Leo, 62, 149, 183
D'Alessio, Lucien, 62, 149, 183
D'Alessio, Pius, 62, 149, 183
D'Alessio, Sixtus, 62, 149, 183
Da Silva, Michael, xiii, 206
Daley, Richard J., 108
Dancy, Jonathan, 110

"A Dangerous Maid" (episode), 8

Danziger, Lucy, 156, 159–160, 165
  contrast with Margaret, 162–63
  relationship with Nucky Thompson, 133, 159–160
  relationship with Van Alden, 32, 82, 87, 123–24, 133–34, 160

Darmody, Angela:
  murder victim, 61, 171–73, 183
  wife of Jimmy, 60–61, 108, 137, 139, 170

Darmody, Gillian, xii–xiii, 156, 163, 165, 166, 168, 169, 171–75
  adult relationship with Commodore Kaestner, 160–61, 166, 167–170, 171
  as Madam/stripper/prostitute, 62, 169
  mother of Jimmy, 57, 62, 91, 97–99, 135, 139, 161, 169–170, 172–73
  murderer, 172–173
  oedipal relationship with Jimmy, 35–37, 43–45, 55, 60, 139, 161, 166, 170, 174
  relationship with Gyp Rosetti, 45, 160–61, 166, 168, 174
  relationship with Lucky Luciano, 160–61, 166, 168
  victim of child rape, 32–33, 57, 91–95, 97–99, 165, 167–170

Darmody, James (Jimmy), 39–40, 42, 56, 63, 111, 172
  as gangster, 71, 101–04, 106, 110, 112, 126–27, 135, 139–141, 145, 167, 169, 183
  husband of Angela, 60–61, 108, 137, 139, 170, 172
  oedipal relationship with Gillian, xiii, 35–37, 43–45, 55, 60, 139, 161, 166, 170, 174
  relationship with Nucky Thompson/Nucky's surrogate son, 4, 9, 29–30, 51, 57, 62–63, 69, 74, 91–93, 95–99, 102–03, 110, 141, 145, 152, 163, 179, 181, 183, 191–92, 202
  relationship with Richard Harrow, 55–62, 106, 131, 137, 140–141
  son of Gillian, 32, 91–93, 95–99, 135, 169, 171, 172, 173
  son of Commodore, 57, 62, 91–93, 95–99, 102, 135, 139–149, 171
  war veteran, xii, 40, 42, 55, 122–23, 129, 131, 135, 137, 140, 145, 170, 173

Darmody, Tommy, 61–62, 141, 161, 171, 173–74

Daugherty, Harry, 70

David Copperfield (Dickens), 52

The Day After (television movie), 78

de Valera, Eamon, 70, 73–74

Debar, Joseph, 122n

Dempsey, Jack, 108

deontology, 146

Department of Internal Revenue, 101

Descartes, René, 26

determinism, 80–81

Detroit, 82
Dewey, Thomas E., 20
Diana, Daughter of Jupiter
  (from mythology), 166
Dickens, Charles, 52
Diekelmann, Nancy, 201n
Dorothy, 59, 61
Dorothy and the Wizard of Oz
  (Baum), 58
Dostoevsky, Fyodor. *See*
  Dostoyevsky, Fyodor
Dostoyevsky, Fyodor, 26, 129
Doyle, Mickey, 28–29, 31
Drucci, Vincent (The Schemer),
  12

Easter, 62, 88, 172
eBay, 185
Educational Researcher, 192n
Egan, Kieran:
  Teaching as Storytelling:
  An Alternative Approach to
  Teaching and Curriculum
  in the Elementary School,
  200n
Eichmann, Adolf, 68
Eig, Jonathan, 71
Eighteenth Amendment. *See*
  National Prohibition Act of
  1919
Elizabethan Age, 120
Elliott, Frederick, 79, 85, 104
"Emerald City" (episode), 58, 127
Emerson, Ralph Waldo, 105
"Enacting Narrative Pedagogy:
  The Lived Experiences of
  Students and Teachers"
  (Andrews, Ironside, Nosek,
  Sims, Swenson, Yeomans,
  Young, and Diekelmann),
  201n

Engels, Frederick, 144
escapism, 132, 134, 138
Estelle (character, *No Exit*), 136
ethical egoism, 145
ethical theory, xii, 145
ethics, 144
  of doing vs. allowing harm,
    91–99
  of lying/deception, xii,
    101–113
  Christian, 29–31
  obligation to truth, 68, 70–78
  of right action, 145
  of the Ten Commandments,
    41
  Victorian, 43
Europe, 122
euthanasia, 93
Euthyphro, 199
evil genius, 26
existential crisis, 131
existentialism, xii, 129–130
"Extreme Violence Cuts Bloody
  Path through Noteworthy
  TV Dramas" (Braxton),
  187n

facticity, 135–36
Fallis, Don, xii, 206
"Family Limitation" (episode),
  160
Fargo (movie), 125
Federal Bureau of Investigation,
  20
feminism, xii
Fisher, Amy, 67
Fitzpatrick, John, xiii, 206
Five Families: The Rise,
  Decline, and Resurgence of
  America's Most Powerful
  Mafia Empires (Rabb), 24n

Five Points Gang, 16
Flamingo Hotel, 10
Florida, 20
Florintine Films, 105
Fogliani, Giovanni, 15
Fourth Ward Republican Club, 16
free will, 87
Freire, Paulo, 199–200, 202
  Pedagogy of the Oppressed, 197, 197n
Freud, Sigmund, xiii, 35–37, 37n, 38–45
  Character and Culture, 37, 37n, 39n, 41
  Civilization and Its Discontents, 41, 42n
  denial, 42
  dreams, 37
  ego, superego, and id, 39
  Eros and Thanatos, 38, 40–41, 43
  everything (purportedly) reduced to sex, 35, 38
  evolutionary process, 38
  Group Psychology and the Analysis of the Ego, 44, 44n
  Oedipus Complex, 35, 43–45
  parricide, 44–45
  psychoanalysis, 36, 43
  rationalization, 42
  Standard Edition, 37, 37n, 43n
  "Thoughts on War and Death", 35
Friedman, Thomas, 185

gangsters. *See* mafia
Garcin, (character, *No Exit*), 136–37
Gates, Bill, 185–86

"Georgia Peaches" (episode), 54, 183
Germany, 144
Gillette razors, 49
"Gimcrack & Bunkum" (episode), 60, 104, 108, 110–11, 137, 183
"Ging, Gang, Goolie" (episode), 62
Glenmore (hunter), 108
Glenn, John 78
God, 25–27, 29–31, 79, 83–84, 86–87, 133–134
  benevolence, 80, 86
  omnipotence, 80–81, 86–87
  process God, 88
  will of God, 79–89
  works in mysterious ways, 84–85
Good Housekeeping, 56
Good Samaritan laws, 94
Google, 77, 185
Graham, Stephen, 71
The Great Hardin, 103
The Great War. *See* World War I
Greek town, 102
Greene, Richard, xii, 206
Grotius, Hugo:
  Law of War and Peace, 103, 110

Halloran, Ray, 111
Hamlet (Shakespeare), 45
Hammonton Woods, 71
happening truth, 193–94
Harding, Warren, 51, 121, 181
Harrow, Richard, xii, 55–63, 98, 106, 108, 131–32, 135, 137–38, 140–41, 173–74, 183

Harvard, 107
Harvey, William, 119
Hazel, Paul, 194, 194n
HBO, 48, 74, 187
Hearst, William Randolph, 19
Heine, Heinrich, 41
Hell, 136–37
Hernman (victim), 183
Hill, William, 183
Himmler, Heinrich, 68
Hirschbein, Ron, xiii, 207
Hobbes, Thomas, 26, 40, 144,
    148, 151
Leviathan, 120, 147–48
"Hold Me in Paradise"
    (episode), 51
Hollingdale, R.J., 31, 31n
Holocaust, 68, 86
The Holocaust (television
    miniseries), 68
"Home" (episode), 9, 56, 59,
    106, 117, 123, 129, 131
Hoover, Herbert, 22
Horvitz, Manny, 61, 183
Houdini, Harry, 103
"How Al Capone Would Run
    This Country" (Vanderbilt),
    22n
"The Human Hippocampus
    and Spatial Episodic
    Memory" (Burgess,
    Maguire, and O'Keefe),
    194n

IBM, 185
Idaho, 172
Indiana, 15, 172
Ines (character, *No Exit*), 136
*The Institutes of the Christian
    Religion* (Calvin), 81, 81n
Intel, 185

*Interactive Learning
    Environments*, 194n
Internal Revenue Service, 20
IRA. *See* Irish Republican
    Army
Ireland, 70, 73–74, 144
Irish Civil War, 73
Irish Government, 70
Irish Republican Army, 72–73,
    180
Ironside, Pamela M., 201n
Irreversible (movie), 183
*Issues and Innovations in
    Nursing Education*, 201n
Italian-Americans, 101
Italy, 4
"The Ivory Tower" (episode),
    9, 124, 127

Jagger, Mick, 40
jazz, 189
Jesus of Nazareth, 41, 88,
    134
Jeunet, Madame, 103, 107–08,
    149, 159
Johnson, Alfred (person on
    whom the character Eli
    Thompson is based), 70
Johnson, Enoch (Nucky)
    (Treasurer of Atlantic City
    on whom the character
    Nucky Thompson is based),
    3–8, 11–12, 16–19, 22–23,
    69, 71, 74–77, 124, 180–81,
    194
Johnson, Nelson, 16, 16n, 18,
    69, 75–76, 180, 180n, 181
Johnson, Smith 11
Julius Caesar (play), 127
Jyllandsposten (newspaper),
    184

Kaestner, Louis (Commodore), 12, 101, 110–11, 173
based on Commodore Kuehnle, 11, 69–70, 74
father of Jimmy, 57, 60, 62, 135, 139–141
gangster, 29, 56, 104, 127, 135, 183
rape of Gillian, 57, 60, 91–97, 99, 161, 167, 171
relationship with Gillian, 160–61, 166–171
relationship with Nucky, 29, 43, 69, 74, 91–97, 99, 102
Kama Sutra, 37
Kant, Immanuel, 105, 144
Lectures on Ethics, 111
"On a Supposed Right to Lie from Altruistic Motives," 102–03
On Education, 198, 198n
Kelly, Paul, 16
Kendall (Chalky White's driver), 195
The Kennedys (television movie), 68
Kessel, Louis (person on whom the character Eddie Kessler is based), 70
Kessler, Eddie, 70, 121
Kierkegaard, Søren, 129
Kingsbury, Maria, xii, 207
KKK. *See* Ku Klux Klan
Ku Klux Klan, 29, 62, 102, 123, 151, 156, 183, 195
Kuehnle, Louis (Commodore) (Mob boss of Atlantic City on whom the character Commodore Kaestner is based), 8, 11, 70, 74–75
Kushner, Harold, 86, 86n, 87

La Belle Femme (boutique), 103
Lansky, Meyer, 6–8, 11, 16, 18, 20, 106
Las Vegas, xi, 10
Last Call: The Rise and Fall of Prohibition (Okrent), 122n
Leviathan, 26, 148
Liam (mobster), 106, 131
Liberty (journal), 22n
Littmann, Greg, xii, 25, 207
Locke, John, 144, 148–151
London, 73
Long Island, 10
The Lord. *See* God
Los Angeles Times, 187n
Lossky, Nikolai, 184
Louise (Angela's friend), 183
Luciano, Charles (Lucky), xi, 3, 6–11, 13, 16, 18, 20, 23, 31, 70, 77, 106, 135, 160, 166, 168, 196, 198
The Lucifer Effect (Zimbardo), 40n
Luther, Martin, 144

MacDonald, Kelly, 181
Machiavelli, Niccolò:
The Prince, xi–xii, 4, 4n, 5–15, 17–23, 25–26, 125–26
mafia, xi–xii, 6, 24n, 25, 31, 69, 76, 103, 124, 143, 180, 183
Magicians' Guild, 103
Maguire, Eleanor A., 194n
Maranzano, Salvatore, 6–10
"Margate Sands" (episode), 62, 174
Marx, Karl H., 144, 151, 185
Masseria, Gieuseppe (Joe the Boss), 6–10
Mauer, Edith, 108
McAllister, Roger, 172–74

McGarricle, John, 71–73
McGarry, Mrs., 124
McManus, George (Hump), 24
McSwiggan, William, 21
Means, Gaston, 5
Mellamphy, Deborah, xiii, 208
Mellon, Andrew, 70
Memorial Day, 137
"Memory Systems of the Brain:
    A Brief History and
    Current Perspective"
    (Squire), 194n
metaphysics, 144
Meursault (character, *The
    Stranger*), 138–39, 141
Mexico, 172
Michael, Charles, 193n
Milgram, Stanley, 39–40, 40n
"The Milkmaid's Lot" (episode),
    62
Mill, John Stuart, 144, 151
Mirkwood, 61
mob. *See* mafia
mobsters. *See* mafia
modern era of philosophy, 144
Monsters Inc. (movie), 125
Montana, 172
morality. *See* ethics
Moran, George (Bugs), 12–13
"Mother Thompson" (episode),
    125
Muhammad, 184
Murena, Lucius Licinius, 118

The National Prohibition Act of
    1919, 16, 107, 149, 200
causes of, xii, 155
consequences of, xi, 3, 5–6, 14,
    29, 69, 76, 101, 128, 130,
    134, 143, 146, 152, 180,
    192

introduction of, xii, 70, 143,
    155, 179, 180
reasons for, 122, 125, 155
repeal of, 19, 145
See also The Volstead Act
Nazi Occupation, 102
Neary, Jim, 62, 101, 183
Nero, 118, 128
Neptune, 36
Neptune, King, 127
*Neurobiology of Learning and
    Memory* (Squire), 194n
Neuron, 194n
New Jersey, 69, 180, 188
New Jersey State Attorney, 107
New Jersey State Supreme
    Court, 16, 76
New York (city), 6, 9, 11, 18, 20,
    70, 72, 121, 196
Nicholas II (Tsar); 108
Nicholson, Julianne, 182
Nietzsche, Friedrich, 41, 129
    Eternal Recurrence, Doctrine
        of, 34
    The Gay Science, 26, 34
    "God is dead", 25–27, 29
    last man, 27, 32
    slave morality, 26, 30, 33
    Superman. *See* Nietzsche,
        Übermensch
    Thus Spake Zarathurtra, 25
    Übermensch. xii, 25–34
    will to power, 32
*Friedrich Nietzsche in Plain
    and Simple English* (book),
    34n
*Nietzsche: the Man and His
    Philosophy* (Hollingdale),
    31n
"Nights in Ballygran"
    (episode), 14, 125, 181
9/11 Commission Report, 68

Nixon (movie), 68
non-identity problem, 98
North Side Gang, 12–13, 21
Nosek, Catherine, 201n
Novick, Lynn, 105
Nuova Villa Tammaro, 7
Nursing and Health Care Perspectives, 201n

O'Banion, Dion, 13
Obedience to Authority (Milgram), 40n
objective violence, 183–85
Odette, prostitute, 56, 58
Oedipus Rex (Sophocles), 45
O'Keefe, John, 194n
Okrent, Daniel, 122n
Oliverotto of Fermo, 15
Olmstead, Roy, 107
omertà, 31
the One, 158
O'Neill, George, 110–11, 183
organized crime. *See* mafia
the Other, 156–58
"Ourselves Alone" (episode), 12, 52, 73, 106, 113, 124
Oz, 61
Oz (television series), 187

Palladino, Aleksa, 183
Palm Island, 20
Parfit, Derek, 96
"Paris Green" (episode), 17, 51, 82, 91–92, 103, 121, 124, 133, 139
Park Central Hotel, 24
passive euthanasia. *see* euthanasia
The Path to 9/11 (television movie), 68

Patton: The Final Days (television movie), 68
Pearl, prostitute, 9, 56, 60–61
"Pedagogy, Virtue, and Narrative Identity in Teaching" (van Manen), 197n
"Peg of Old" (episode), 9, 126–27
Pete (hunter), 108
Philadelphia, 195
Philadelphia Inquirer, 113
Philosophy Bites, 110
Pietrusza, David, 16n
Pilate, Pontius, 126
pilot episode. *See* "Boardwalk Empire" (pilot episode)
Pine Barrens, 106
Pitt, Michael, 179
Polay, McCall, 43, 43n, 44
polio, 117
Plato, xii, 38
  Crito, 197
  Euthyphro, 197, 199
  Forms, theory of, 166–67, 169, 171–73
  Ideas, theory of. *See* Plato, Forms, Theory of
  Phaedo, 165–67
  Recollection, theory of, 168
  Republic, 25, 193
  Symposium, 39
  tripartite soul, 39, 166–67
political philosophy, xii
Poyner, Leslie, 193n
President, United States, 181
Princeton, 98, 145, 170, 174
problem of evil, 79–89
process theism, 87–88
prohibition. *See* The National Prohibition Act of 1919
Prohibition (movie), 105, 108

Prohibition era, 18, 72, 75, 145, 148, 191, 202
Prohibition: Its Relationship to Temperance, Good Morals, and Sound Government (Debar), 122n
Protestant Reformation, 144
providential theology, 80, 82, 84, 86
Purcell, Theo, 195
Purnsley, Dunn, 52–53

Rabb, Selwyn, 24n
Ragtime, 187
Randall the Chameleon, 125
Randolph, Esther, 54, 182
The Reagans (television movie), 68
Reformation Era, 81
Remus, George, 127
Republican County Committee, 16
Republican Party, 75–76, 180, 182
"Resolution" (episode), 61
"A Return to Normalcy" (episode), 3, 50, 55, 91, 102, 127, 179
The Right Stuff (movie), 78
Ritz Carlton, 16, 19, 28, 70
The Road to Oz (Baum), 51
Robin Hood, 18
Robison-Greene, Rachel, xii, 208
Rockwell, Norman, 40
Rolling Stone (magazine), 43
Rolls Royce, 19
Roman Catholic doctrine, 86
Roman Empire, 7, 127
Rome, ancient, 118–19, 126
Rooney, Ted, 72

Roosevelt Administration, 19
Rosetti, Gyp, 28–31, 42, 45, 71, 88–89, 141, 160–161, 165, 168, 174, 181, 183
Rousseau, John-Jacques, 144, 148, 150–51
Discourse on the Origin of Equality, 149
Rothstein, Arnold (The Brain), xi, xii, 6, 8–9, 16, 18, 23–24, 28–29, 31, 70, 77, 101–02, 106, 109, 112–13, 124, 135, 183, 194, 196–203
Rothstein: The Life, Times, and Murder of the Criminal Genius Who Fixed the 1919 World Series (Pietrusza), 16
Russian Orthodox Church, 184
The Ryan White Story (television movie), 67

S&M, 174
Sagorsky, Julia, 62
Sagorsky, Paul, 62
Saint Patrick's Day Celtic Dinner, 181
Salon.com, 186
Sartre, Jean-Paul, 130, 135–36, 156
No Exit (play), 136–37
Sawicki (agent), 79
Scalise, John, 15
Schopenhauer, Arthur, 32
scotch, 102, 122
Schroeder, Emily, 54, 58, 107–08, 117, 121, 124
Schroeder, Hans, 32, 74, 109, 145–46, 159, 162, 181
Schroeder, Margaret, 73, 81, 86, 133, 149, 156, 159–160, 162, 165

mother of Emily, 51, 124
mother of Teddy, 51, 124, 150
pursuit of happiness, 49–58,
    63
unseemly behavior/bad
    character, 38, 54, 103,
    107–08, 111, 146, 151
wife of Hans Schoreder, 32,
    74, 181
wife/significant other of
    Nucky hompson, 17, 30, 32,
    43–45, 51, 74, 117, 145,
    163, 193
Schroeder, Theodore (Teddy),
    51, 58, 117, 121, 124, 150
Schwanebeck, Wieland, xiii,
    208
Scorsese, Martin, 69, 186–87
Seattle, 107
Sebso (agent), 29, 37, 82–83,
    101, 104, 107, 124, 133
Seitz, Matt Zoller, 186, 186n
Seneca, 126
    De Clementia, 118–120,
    126
The Sermon on the Mount, 41
Shakespeare, William, 119
Shakespearean, 127
Sheridan, Charlie, 9, 101–02,
    104, 106
Sheriff, Atlantic County, 181
Showalter, Carl, 125
Sickles, Victor, 183
Siegel, Benjamin (Bugsy),
    10–11
Sims, Sharon L., 201n
Sinn Féin, xi, 72–73
Sirvent, Roberto, xii, 208
situated freedom, 158
Slator, Owen, 73, 162
Social Contract Theory, xiii, 31,
    146, 148–49

Socrates, 197, 199
Sondheim, Steven, 61
Soprano, Tony, 43
The Sopranos (television
    series), 69, 77, 186–87
Sorenson, Roy, 111–12
Soros, George, 185–86
Soviet Union, 78, 184
"Spaghetti and Coffee"
    (episode), 5
Squire, Larry R., 194n
SS, 68, 102, 110
St. Gregory's Award, 182
St. Valentine's Day Massacre of
    1929, 21
Stanford University, 40
State of Nature, 40, 144,
    147–49
Steinman, Lolly, 113
stoicism, 118
story truth, 193–94
"Storytelling as Pedagogy:
    An Unexpected Outcome of
    Narrative Inquiry"
    (Coulter, Michael, and
    Poyner), 193n
strong providential theology.
    See providential theology
subjective violence, 182–83,
    187
Suffragette Movement, xi
"Sunday's Best" (episode), 62,
    88, 173
Swenson, Melinda M., 201n
symbolic violence, 184
systemic violence, 184–85,
    189

Temperance League. *See*
    Women's Temperance
    League

Temperance Movement. *See*
Women's Temperance
Movement
Temperance Society. *See*
Women's Temperance
League
Texas Chainsaw Massacre
(movie), 37
theology, 80
Thompson, Elias (Eli), 17, 51,
91, 101, 109–111, 127, 151,
167, 174, 181, 183
Thompson gun, 21
Thompson, Margaret. *See*
Schroeder, Margaret
Thompson, Eliza, 125
Thompson, Enoch Malachi
(Nucky), 70–71, 87, 133,
150, 159–161, 174, 188,
193
based on Nucky Johnson, 69,
74, 76–77, 180, 194
businessman, 38, 42, 70, 73,
149
facilitating Gillian's rape,
91–97, 99, 166, 168
gangster, 5, 8–9, 20, 22–25,
29–32, 36–37, 42, 45, 50,
54, 56, 73, 86, 88, 91, 99,
101–04, 108–110, 112–13,
118, 123, 125–26, 139, 141,
145–46, 148–49, 151–52,
162–63, 181–83, 188–89
good citizen, 17, 180
exhibiting good
hygiene/snappy dresser,
117–18, 123–24, 126, 188
Husband/significant other of
Margaret Schroeder, 30,
32, 38, 43, 51–54, 58, 74,
103, 107–08, 117, 146,
159–160, 162–63, 181

hypocrite, 38, 123, 170, 182,
186
Jimmy's father figure, 9, 42,
51, 57, 60, 74, 91, 103,
139–141, 145, 152, 169, 171
Nietzschean
Superman/Übermensch,
xii, 25–34
Machiavellian prince, xii, 4
moral agent, 41–43
politician, xii, 30, 52, 69, 86,
91, 101–02, 107, 117–121,
123, 127, 146, 152,
179–182, 191–92
psychological states of, 37,
39–41
public speaker, 3, 14, 29, 30,
69, 101–02, 105, 109, 125,
162, 179, 191–92, 194,
199–200, 202–03
pursuit of pleasure, 49–53,
55–56, 63
Tin Soldier, 59
The Tin Soldier (Bailey), 59
Tin Woodman, 58–59
"To the Lost" (episode), 54, 62,
86, 127, 140, 182–83
Tolkien, J.R.R., 61
Tom Sawyer (Twain), 52
Torrio, Johnny (The Fox), 6, 8,
11, 13, 15–16, 18, 23, 70,
72, 101, 104
"Toward a Narrative Pedagogy
for Interactive Learning
Environments" (Hazel),
194n
transcendence, 135–36
Trenton, 148
truthiness, 78
"21" (episode), 55, 102, 123,
169
21 Club (nightclub), 20

"Two Boats and a Lifeguard"
  (episode), 127

"Under God's Power She
  Flourishes" (episode), 22,
  111, 170
Underground Man, 26
United States Government, 78
United States of America, 78,
  123, 127, 128
"Using Narrative Pedagogy:
  Learning and Practicing
  Interpretative Thinking"
  (Ironside), 201n

Van Alden, Nelson, 28, 38, 70,
  103–04, 107, 112, 148
  Agent, 9, 20, 29, 130, 148
  disgraced agent, 29, 36, 39,
    127, 138
  husband of Rose Van Alden,
    36, 37, 70, 133
  hypocrite, 36–39
  murderer of Sebso, 29, 124,
    133
  Relationship with Lucy
    Danziger, 32, 37, 82, 123,
    133, 159–160
  religious, xii, 29, 36, 79–83,
    85–89, 133
Van Alden, Rose, 82, 123–24, 134
van Manen, Max, 197n, 199
Vanderbilt, Cornelius, Jr., 22n
The Volstead Act, xi, 29,
  128,143, *see also* The
  National Prohibition Act of
  1919

Wahlberg, Mark, 69, 187

Wal-Mart, 145
Waldorf Towers, 20
War Memorial. *See* Atlantic
  City War Memorial
Washington (state), 107
Washington, D.C., 148
*Washington: Behind Closed
  Doors* (television movie),
  78
Water Commission, 75
Weis, Earl (Hymie), 12, 13
Wiesel, Elie, 68
Weiss Family, 68
Western philosophy, 130
"What does the Bee Do?"
  (episode), 61, 124, 161,
  166
*When Bad Things Happen to
  Good People* (Kushner),
  86
Whigham, Shea, 181
wine, 18, 122, 167, 174, 207
whiskey, xiii, 18, 70, 73,
  101–02, 17, 122, 124, 180,
  189
White, Albert (Chalky), xii, 30,
  43, 49–50, 52–53, 55–56,
  62–63, 102, 119, 123, 151,
  181–83, 195, 200, 203
White, Lenore, 52
Whitney, William, 107
Williams, Michael Kenneth,
  181
Wilson, Woodrow, 11
Winslow, Billy, 101
Winter, Terence, 69, 77, 187
Wizard of Oz, 59
Women's Christian
  Temperance Union, 105,
  117, 119, 122–23, 146
Women's Temperance
  Movement, xii, 125

Women's Temperance League, 29, 38, 105, 124–25, 162, 179, 182, 191, 202

Women's Temperance League of Atlantic City. *See* Women's Temperance League

Women's Temperance Union. *See* Women's Christian Temperance Union

Wood, Grant, 123

The Works of James Arminius, Volume 2, 84

World Series, 19

World Series (1919), 8, 102

World Trade Center attacks, 68

World War I, xii, 40, 55, 123, 129, 144–45, 170

World War II, 129

Yale, Frankie, 196, 198, 200–02

Yeomans, Patricia K., 201n

Young, Patricia K., 201n

Zimbardo, Philip, 39–40, 40n

Žižek, Slavoj, 183–184, 187, 189, *Violence: Six Sideways Reflections*, 182, 182n, 184–88, 189

"Nobody Has to Be Vile, 185–86

Printed in the USA
CPSIA information can be obtained
at www.ICGtesting.com
JSHW012025140824
68134JS00033B/2883